Tofu
GOURMET CUISINE

Frances Boyte
Dietician/Author

Delicious recipes from the
four corners of the world

Dillon Publishing Inc.

National Library of Canada Cataloguing in Publication

Boyte, Frances
     Tofu gourmet cuisine : delicious recipes from the four corners of the
world / Frances Boyte ; translated by Ed and Marilyn Bell.
Translation of: Le tofu international.
Includes bibliographical references and index.
ISBN 0-9732637-0-9
     1. Cookery (Tofu) I. Title.
TX814.5.T63B6913 2003   641.6'5655   C2003-906468-9

Photography:
Roger Côté
Photo styling:
Marie-Chantal Lepage
Translated by:
Ed and Marilyn Bell
Graphics by:
John Caco

Legal Deposit: National Library of Canada, 4th quarter, 2003
ISBN: 0-9732637-0-9

Published by:
Dillon Publishing Inc.
7-919 Fraser Dr.
Burlington, ON
Canada L7L 4X8
Telephone: 905.637.2317
Facsimile: 905.634.2776
www.dillonpublishing.com
info@dillonpublishing.com

Printed in Canada by:
Battlefield Graphics Inc.
Burlington, ON CANADA

By the same author:
La magie du tofu, (Yvon Tremblay), Les éditions internationales Alain Stanké Itée, 1982
le TOFU International, Les éditions internationales Alain Stanké Itée, 2001

Tofu
GOURMET CUISINE

To my mother, Denise, who has always supported me in my personal and professional life.

To my sons, Philippe and Olivier, who held the fort.... and sometimes more.

And a special thank you to my sister Nancy who introduced me to my English team! Ed and Marilyn Bell who translated the book from the French text; John Caco from Dillon Publishing who created the layout; and my publisher, Tom Dillon of Dillon Publishing Inc., whose vision of the project inspired our team to succeed.

"Alexandre"
Photo by:
Jocelyne Jacques (JOQUE)

Tofu
GOURMET CUISINE

ACKNOWLEDGEMENTS

One great book.....One great team!

The publication of this book was made possible by the collaboration of a team of highly dedicated people. I would like to express my sincere gratitude to all those people who worked with me to produce "Tofu Gourmet Cuisine".

Special thanks to my sister, Nancy Boyte, who introduced me to my translators, Ed and Marilyn Bell of Campbell River, British Columbia. My sister's involvement created the extraordinary momentum which led to the collaboration and success of the team.

Ed and Marilyn did their work with great skill and patience. I especially thank them for their positive support at the beginning of this adventure. It was themselves, after all, who introduced me to Tom Dillon (Dillon Publishing Inc.) of Burlington, Ontario. Tom is a very dynamic publisher and his support has been most important to the life of this book. Thanks to Tom and his team; and a very special thank you to John Caco, who created the style of this book.

Thank you to all of the chefs who participated in this project to create the wonderful gourmet recipes and to my friends who joined in by contributing their own successful tofu recipes. A very special thank you to Roger Côté, a well known Quebec photographer and Marie-Chantal Lepage, executive chef of the Manoir Montmorency (Quebec) who produced the beautiful photos. Marie-Chantal has stylized the recipes as no one else could and Roger has signed these great food pictures.

Many thanks also to Eileen Bell of Edmonton, Alberta, for her dedicated work as media liaison director for this book. Thank you also to Yves Pelletier (Renaud & Cie) in Quebec and Marie-Lucie Crépeau (Boutique Terre et Mer) in Quebec, who offered us the beautiful dishes for the photos.

My thanks to this great team, located across Canada, for their positive support and determination as we worked together to bring you "Tofu Gourmet Cuisine".

Frances Boyte

Frances Boyte

Table of Contents

Tofu
GOURMET CUISINE

A NOTE FROM THE AUTHOR

I have written this book to share the idea that tofu, a food with countless possibilities, can be as highly popular in Western cuisine as it has been in Eastern cuisine for more than a thousand years. In addition to the health benefits of including tofu in your diet, I believe that the popularity of tofu will increase from the pleasurable dining experiences it can provide.

Tofu is not just found in the traditional daily diet of the Asian people, it is also highly valued at their banquet tables. As you will find, the incomparable versatility of tofu brings with it the promise of original discoveries and experiences from appetizers through the main meal to desserts! It is a food that will lead you magnificently and easily into a world of exploration and creative culinary adventure.

I also intend this book to be a counterweight against the western myths that tofu is a mundane food which only has a place in vegetarian diets or whose primary asset is as an economic substitute for meat. Tofu is much more than that!

Tofu Gourmet Cuisine

Tofu Gourmet Cuisine complements my passion for travel and learning about different cultures. It allows me to bring you new and exciting cuisine from the four corners of the world. I feel that globalization has stimulated a growing interest in all of the traditions of the world, including food and food preparation. This blending of cultures has given rise to the emergence of fusion cuisine.

This book is for everyone, master chefs and amateurs alike: those passionate about the art of cooking, as well as those who simply love to cook. Tofu Gourmet Cuisine will guide you towards new culinary horizons.

Is Tofu a health food?

Tofu is acclaimed for its nutritional value. It is one of the richest sources of protein available. It has absolutely no cholesterol. It is also a great source of vitamins and minerals, including calcium and iron. Just imagine the benefits in your diet... It would reduce the worrisome prospects of obesity, diabetes, heart problems and certain forms of cancer. By reducing your intake of animal fat, your metabolism will reward you with a higher energy level and a more healthy appearance.

After thirty years of working in both private practice and tailoring individual nutrition programs in corporate settings, I know that one "universal diet" does not suit everyone. A healthy food plan must not only take into account widely accepted scientific standards but must also, in my opinion, be personalized according to an individual's needs, objectives, and values. I also believe that pleasure in eating is a basic ingredient of any good diet.

How I wrote Tofu Gourmet Cuisine

I wrote this book in close collaboration with five chefs, each of whom has a different culinary style and their own particular interest in the traditions and specialties of the world. Éric Boutin, Sébastien Leblond, Marie-Chantal Lepage, Benoît Paquet, and José Trottier, all of whom I will introduce to you later in this book. Each one has enthusiastically accepted the challenge presented by Tofu Gourmet Cuisine. It is with great pleasure that I invite you to enjoy the recipes that they have shared in this book. Their know-how, their sophistication and their love of innovation offer savoury, attractive and original food for all tastes. Tofu Gourmet Cuisine also contains recipes from friends and other chefs who have long embraced the pleasures of tofu.

You will see that tofu is not only for health enthusiasts. By introducing it into your daily eating, and including it in your festive meals, it will bring you new gourmet experiences.

I invite you to try my recipes, which will inspire you and satisfy your culinary desires.

Bon appétit,
   Frances Boyte

Tofu
GOURMET CUISINE

Part One:

The art and tools of making tofu

By FRANCES BOYTE

Tofu
GOURMET CUISINE

How to Make Homemade Tofu

The preparation of homemade tofu contains 4 steps:

Soaking of the soybeans
Making soy milk
Coagulating soy milk
Pressing the tofu

Preparation time: about one hour after soaking the soybeans.
Portion: 2 cups or 500 ml of dried soybeans yields about 1 pound or 500 g of tofu.

Ingredients:
2 cups or 500 ml dried soybeans
water
2 tsp. epsom salts (coagulant)**

*** The coagulant is a salt or an acid ingredient. The agent that is traditionally used is nigari, an extract of sea salt. Other agents that are used to promote coagulation are: magnesium sulfate (Epsom salts), calcium chloride, calcium sulphate (gypsum), vinegar and either lemon or lime juice. The texture and flavour of the tofu vary depending on which coagulant is used. The coagulant that is chosen will likewise have an effect on the ultimate nutritional value of the tofu that you make.*

Method:
SOAKING THE SOYBEANS
   Rinse the soybeans and cover them with enough water to allow them to expand. Let them soak for at least 6 hours and preferably for more than 12 hours. Rinse them well in fresh water and drain thoroughly.

MAKING SOY MILK
   In a blender, crush the soybeans to a purée by adding 3 cups or 750 ml of hot, but not boiling water to 1 cup or 500 ml of beans. Pour the purée into a saucepan and cook on medium heat for 10 minutes, while stirring constantly. This stage of the process is very important as the cooking is needed to "destroy the enzyme" that inhibits the effective digestion of soy protein by humans. Strain the mixture through a cheesecloth to separate the soy milk from the okara.***

*   ***OKARA: The pulp that remains in the cheesecloth is called okara. It has little flavour but is rich in nutritional value. It is used with other ingredients in various cooked dishes. As an example, okara is able to be used to replace some of the flour in bakery products.*

COAGULATING SOY MILK
   Heat the soy milk until it reaches a slow boil. When the milk is hot, add one third of the coagulant after it has been dissolved in cold water, then stir. Pour in the rest of the dissolved coagulant and stir again. Set aside. After about 15 to 20 minutes, the curds will float to the surface as a result of the coagulation. Gently scoop the curds from the tip of the whey and ladle them into a forming container lined with cheesecloth in order to "drain" any leftover whey. Now you have tofu!

PRESSING THE TOFU
   Wrap the well drained tofu in cheesecloth and place in a container. Place a small weight on the lid of the container and allow to sit for 15 to 30 minutes, depending on the degree of firmness that you want. The resulting firmness usually depends on the amount of weight that you have used as a press. Withdraw the cheesecloth and deposit the resulting tofu into a container filled with cold water. Allow it to sit for another hour before eating or using for cooking.

TREMBLAY (Yvon) & BOYTE (Frances). La magie du tofu : 80 recettes simples et économiques, Éditions Alain Stanké, 1982.

What is tofu?

What Is Tofu?

Tofu is a product derived from the soybean.
TO means " bean " and FU refers to " curds ".

The soybean is the only leguminous plant from which a milk-like liquid, soymilk, can be extracted. The process of making tofu is similar to making cheese. When a coagulant is added to soymilk, the liquid separates into curds and whey. Tofu is the curd produced by this process.

Its History

Tofu originated in China more than 2000 years ago. A detailed history of this food would require a book of its own. This section gives only a brief summary of its history from its discovery in the 1st century B.C. to the present day.

There are two theories as to the origin of tofu. The first one speculates that the process to develop tofu was discovered after some soymilk curdled due to neglect. Experimentation with the resulting substance led to trying it as a possible food source. The second theory advances the idea that the Chinese, who generally did not use farm animals for their milk, applied the cheese making procedures of their southern neighbours, the Indians, and their northern neighbours, the Mongolians, to soymilk. This latter possibility is more probable because both the Indian and the Mongolian cultures understood the cheese making process.

Reference to tofu is made in the historic Chinese writings of the 6th century. It had already traveled to Japan by the 8th century and was most likely introduced to upper class Japanese society by Buddhist monks. At a later date it was found to be part of the food culture of the general population. According to popular belief, the discovery of tofu (known as doufu in Chinese) is attributed to Liu An, a Chinese scholar, philosopher and politician who was also drawn to Taoist meditation and scientific experimentation.

Buddhism prescribes a light diet, exempt of meat for its adherents. Tofu, thus, became an acceptable, alternate source of protein.

From a culinary point of view, the current use of tofu today has evolved over the centuries into many forms. Certain types of tofu have disappeared and others have been created. Today many varieties of tofu are used in Asiatic foods and they have begun to be used in the West as well.

Tofu has been a part of the culture of the Orient for a long time. Besides its role as a main food, it is often used in certain rites and ceremonies (Tea masters use it in special tea ceremonies). Reference to it is found in poetry, popular expressions, and proverbs. Presently, Westerners aware of research and findings of the past fifteen years are adopting tofu as a healthy protein source. I personally hope that you will choose it also for its gourmet possibilities.

Varieties of Tofu:

Many varieties of tofu are available on the Eastern market. The most popular ones on the Western market are:

Regular

Silken

Ready to eat tofu

Dessert tofu

Fried tofu

Regular tofu:

Looks like a block of white cheese. It comes as firm or semi-firm. It is sold fresh in a plastic container filled with water or vacuum-packed. This tofu comes natural or seasoned with herbs or seaweed.

Fresh tofu has a taste to remember...! And, of course, there is nothing better than "homemade" tofu (see recipe - page 12). Fresh tofu is best described as a soft pressed tofu.

Silken tofu (Japanese style)

Has a softer and creamier texture than the regular variety. It resembles custard or yogurt. It is sold in Tetra-Pak packaging. The advantage of this container is that you can store your tofu on the pantry shelf until you open it and then it has to go in the refrigerator.

There is a difference in the making of these two types of tofu. The regular tofu curd is pressed into cakes after a coagulant is added. Whereas, in the making of silken tofu a thicker soymilk is used with the coagulant . Lactone is then added to the preparation to form the tofu cake without pressing it.

It is interesting to know that the coagulant and the process used in the manufacturing of tofu will impact on its nutritional value and you should be aware of these differences. When you see calcium sulfate on the ingredient list of the product, your tofu is the richest in calcium. It is important to take into account these differences but not to be obsessed by them. "Play it by taste also".

Ready to eat tofu:

These varieties of tofu are generally marinated, cooked and presented in a sauce ready to serve.

Dessert tofu:

Soft tofu seasoned with fruit ready to serve as such, or as a part of a recipe.

Fried tofu:

This tofu has a distinct flavour and a more substantial character. Its texture is similar to meat, especially poultry. It is often used as a meat substitute. I suggest adding it to your sushi as a treat ! (See recipes for sushi : page 44)

Tofu
GOURMET CUISINE

Where do we get Tofu?

You should be able to easily find all varieties of tofu described above in the Chinese and Asian specialty food shops, health food stores and in most supermarkets.

How to use tofu?

"From appetizers, to main meals, to desserts!"

Tofu is one of the most versatile foods in existence. One of its most important characteristics is its capacity to absorb flavors. This "chameleon" like quality is what makes tofu so perfect as a companion to other foods and as a creative ingredient for the chef. We also say that tofu behaves like a sponge, which is one of the main reasons that it is so easily adaptable in recipes from around the world, like those that you will discover in "Tofu Gourmet Cuisine".

Regular tofu and silken tofu have been used in the recipes of this book. Regular tofu is best used as cubes and slices. It goes very well in sautéed, grilled and baked dishes. Silken tofu is best used in dressings and mayonnaise, sauces, creamy desserts and smoothies. You can subtly introduce tofu to everyone by using silken tofu in desserts such as strawberry mousse or crème brûlée. (see recipes page 108)

You can use fresh tofu to make a sautéed dish if you are very careful with it and silken tofu to make cubes if you do not shake them. Silken tofu comes as soft, firm or extra firm. However, the extra firm silken tofu is still soft compared to the regular tofu.

Fried tofu should be boiled to remove any excess oil before using it in a recipe.

How to store tofu?

All tofu, except that contained in unopened Tetra-Paks, has to be kept in the refrigerator. Fried tofu is kept in the refrigerator without water. The water with fresh tofu is changed daily. The vacuum packed and the Tetra-Pak tofu are kept in water, once opened, the water then must be changed every day. Conservation time for your tofu once in the water is approximately 3 days for best results.

In the Orient, tofu is a food for connoisseurs! Now, it is up to you to explore and treat your palate to the exquisite possibilities of tofu.

Tofu and Health

Tofu
GOURMET CUISINE

The Soybean

The soybean, the chief ingredient of tofu, is the most nutritious legume. It is a noteworthy source of protein, rich in minerals and vitamins. This legume contains more fat than any other legume; however, it is low in saturated fat and well balanced between polyunsaturated and monounsaturated fat. The goal in one's diet is not to avoid fat but to choose the right quality and amount of fat. Furthermore, tofu's content in phytoestrogens makes it a very effective food in alleviating the symptoms of menopause.

And now...Tofu

Over the centuries, Asians have experimented with the soybean and made many different kinds of food from it. Some of these food products are renowned for their versatility and tastiness from a culinary point of view; others are highly prized for their excellent nutrients and for the positive effects that they bestow on our health. The creativity of Asians in utilizing the soybean is particularly evident in their culinary repertoire. Three products are considered the backbone of their cuisine: tofu, miso (fermented soy paste with interesting nutritional value) and shoyu or tamari (soy sauce). Tofu is a very substantial food that advantageously replaces the meat in one's food plan.

The nutritional value of one slice of tofu of 115 g or 4 ounces
(6 cm x 4 cm x 4 cm)
(2.5 inches x 1.5 inches x 1.5 inches)

KILOJOULES[1]: 366

Proteins	9.3 g		
Glucose[3]	2.2 g		
Lipids[4] (total)	5.5 g		
Saturated fatty acids	0.8 g		
Mono-unsaturated fatty acids	1.22 g		
Poly-unsaturated fatty acids	3.11 g		
Linoleic acid (C 18 : 2)	2.74 g		
Linolenic acid (C 18 : 3)	0.37 g		
Insoluble fibre (fib- i)	——		
Total fibre (fib-t)	0.8 g		
Cholesterol (chol)	——		
Magnesium (Mg)	35 mg		
Calcium (Ca)	403 mg		
Phosphorous (P)	112 mg		
Iron (Fe)	6.17 mg		

KILOCALORIES[2]: 87

Zinc (Zn)	0.92 mg
Potassium (K)	139 mg
Sodium (Na)	8 mg
Copper (Cu)	0.222 mg
Manganese (Mn)	0.696 mg
Vitamin A	10 RE
Thiamine (B-1)	0.09 mg
Riboflavin (B-2)	0.06 mg
Total niacin (nia-t)	2.6 NE
Pantothenic acid (pant)	0.08 mg
Pyridoxine (B-6)	0.054 mg
Cobalamin (B-12)	——
Folacin (fol)	17.3 mcg
Vitamin C	——

1. Kilojoules: unit of measurement for energy in the metric system.
2. Kilocalories: unit of measurement for energy in the imperial system.
3. Glucose: synonymous with sugar.
4. Lipid: synonymous with fat.

NE = niacin equivalent   g = grams   mg = milligrams   mcg = micrograms

Source: BRAULT DUBUC (Micheline) et CARON LAHAIE (Liliane).
"Valeur nutritive des aliments", Éd.Société Brault-Lahaie, 8e édition, Québec, Canada, 1998.

You should be aware that:

The protein content of tofu varies from 10 to 15 g per 100 g according to the firmness of the product.

The calcium content varies following the coagulant used from 200 mg to 700 mg per 100 g. The firmness will also create a small variation.

The iron content will also vary from 5 to 10 mg per 100 g in accordance with the firmness of the product. The nutritional value of the soybeans used does, of course, influence the final product. Organic soybeans are not genetically modified.

What to make of these nutritional values?

As the soybean, tofu is a rich source of protein. The quality of its protein had not been fully recognized for its fair value up until recently, whereby researchers agreed to award it a perfect protein score, the same given to milk and egg.

---

1 portion of 100 g of tofu
(15 g of protein) equals 1 cup of red kidney beans or 1/2 cup of soybeans

---

1 portion of 100 g of tofu
(680 mg of calcium) equals to 2 glasses of milk of 8 ounces

---

1 portion of tofu has at least 2 or 3 times more iron than ground beef
(according to the type of tofu used).

Fat and cholesterol
Tofu, unlike other sources of animal protein, has a very low content of saturated fat and a good balance between polyunsaturated and monounsaturated fat. Furthermore, it has no cholesterol. Tofu presents us with a healthy alternative. By introducing tofu into your diet, you can cut back on your consumption of animal fat and thereby help yourself with the prevention of obesity, cardio-vascular problems, and certain forms of cancer.

Minerals and Vitamins
Tofu is a good source of minerals. It contains a good amount of iron and its high calcium content helps to prevent osteoporosis. It also has an interesting and varied composition of vitamins.

Calories
Tofu is good for your immediate health and for your longevity. Its low caloric content makes it an ideal food for those who want to have a leaner physique but do not wish to sacrifice their nutritional intake.

Other Characteristics of Tofu

In addition to its nutritional value, tofu has other significant benefits such as its alkaline composition, its glycemic index; and its effect on cholesterol, digestion and menopause.

The fact that tofu has an alkaline composition is quite significant. Unlike tofu, many protein rich foods such as meat are high in acid content. Including or increasing your consumption of tofu helps to maintain a healthy ph balance.

It has a low Glycemic Index

The Glycemic Index measures the degree and the speed that your blood sugar reaches when you eat or drink a particular food. As this process has an effect on your state of health, it is therefore preferable to eat foods such as tofu that have a low Glycemic Index.

Its effect on Cholesterol

Research shows the good effect of tofu on cholesterol. In fact, tofu lowers the bad element of cholesterol (LDL), the triglycerides, and increases the good element of cholesterol (HDL).

It is Easy to Digest

For people experiencing difficulty digesting their food, tofu is a solution worth trying. Tofu is an excellent food for young and old and those who are convalescing.

It is a Natural Ally in the Struggle with Menopause

Tofu and soy products are natural allies in the struggle with menopause because they contain phytoestrogens, which are hormones derived from a vegetable source. Isoflavones or similioestrogens help reduce the frequency and severity of certain menopausal symptoms like hot flashes and sweats. It has also been observed that Oriental women, who eat these products regularly, have less difficulty with menopause than Western women as well as less breast cancer.

One Last Word !

The nutritional value of tofu and its positive effects on health makes it a front line food in everyone's diet and a great food to enjoy with friends.

Frances Boyte

FRANCES BOYTE
BIOGRAPHY

Dietician and a member of the Order of Professional Dieticians of Quebec.

A visionary, Frances Boyte realized very early in her career that tofu was going to be an extremely important source of food for the health and well being of people in the third millennium. As far back as 1982, she collaborated with chef Yvon Tremblay to write their successful book (The Magic of Tofu) *La magie du tofu*.

Frances Boyte's approach places dietetics into the center of a journey that closely links healthful eating to the pleasures of eating, to the sensuality of foods and to the world of endless colours and flavours. She has long understood that while foods have an influence on the physical health of people, they have an equally important role to play with our mental health. After 30 years of working in both hospitals and private practice, she is convinced that properly selected foods are important in restoring the body to good health and developing the full potential of each person.

For the past ten years, Frances Boyte has developed individualized nutritional programs for her clients in corporate settings, which decreases their rate of absenteeism and helps to prevent "burn-out".

In every day life Frances Boyte is a dietician who seeks out the pleasures of life and finds great satisfaction in contributing to the realization of dreams and to the achievement of the objectives that she sets with her clients as they travel on the path to good health. In the pursuit of good nutritional access for everyone, Frances Boyte is now a consultant for *Les Supermarchés Metro Gagnon*, Quebec, Canada, for the development and marketing of their organic products.

In her clinic, Frances treats people who have stressful careers and heavy responsibilities. She accompanies them on their journeys as they discover the positive effects of wholesome food on their health.

"Eat better.....for a better life"

This is Frances Boyte's winning formula for good health and happiness.

Montmorency...
....and its Chef

MARIE-CHANTAL LEPAGE

The Manoir Montmorency, a prestigious establishment located in the heartland of Quebec, is proud of its renowned reputation in the culinary arts and it is equally proud to feature Mme. Marie-Chantal Lepage as its Executive Chef.

A native Quebecer, Mme. Lepage has worked in the field of fine cuisine since the age of sixteen. Like many of the world's greatest chefs, she is to a large degree, self taught. She challenged her creativity and honed her skills by being employed in such exclusive restaurants as the Maison Serge Bruyère, the Bastille, Chez Bahüaud and the Melrose. Since 1994, Marie-Chantal's creations have been savored at the Manoir Montmorency which boasts the finest of Quebec cuisine, which is made from local products.

One of only a few female chefs in the province of Quebec and the only one in the Quebec City area, Mme. Lepage has already achieved a high level of recognition in the culinary world. She has won several awards, including a gold medal at an International culinary competition in Saskatchewan in 1998. This coming October, she will be participating in La Coupe Des Nations, an international event which will be held at the Quebec City Fair Center. In addition to her duties at the Manoir Montmorency, Mme. Lepage also uses her talents and knowledge to teach future chefs at the Wilbrod-Bhérer School of Quebec.

During the summer of 1997, the Manoir Montmorency and Chef Marie-Chantal Lepage hosted the "Les Chefs Des Chefs" club. This select club is a gathering of all of the prominent chefs, as well as royalty and the heads of state from around the world. This visit was the first of its kind to be hosted in Canada. Mme. Lepage has also represented Quebec and the Manoir Montmorency in Japan during the Festival of International Cuisine which was held at the "Okura Hotel", Tokyo's finest hotel. For almost one month, Mme. Lepage was able to display the richness and flavours of the finest Quebec cuisine. Her participation in this event resulted in a great deal of positive publicity for the Manoir Montmorency and the region of Quebec. In March, 2001, Marie-Chantal was at the Kendall Culinary College in Chicago to demonstrate Quebec cuisine and to participate at a benefit dinner for the Poor Children Brothers at the Drake Hotel. In March, 2002, she was in San Francisco to promote Quebec culinary products at le Grand Café restaurant. While she was there, she did some demonstration recipes for the Association of Women Chefs of the United States.

Only in her mid thirties, Mme. Lepage has already won numerous honors and trophies as a highly qualified chef and organizer of special culinary events. In July, 2003, she represented Canada in Beirut, Lebanon, at the Inter-Continental Vendôme Hotel. The Société des Chefs Cuisiniers et Pâtissiers du Québec elected Mme. Lepage as its Regional Chef of the Year in January, 2000. On May 21, 2000, she was elected National Chef of the Year, making her the first woman to ever receive this honor.

JOSÉ TROTTIER

José Trottier completed his education at Calixa-Lavallée, where, incidentally, he has been teaching foundational chefs' skills for the past three years. José began his career at the Château Champlain and at the Sheraton Center in Montreal. In 1990, he was preparing desserts at the Le Point de Vue restaurant under the direction of Mr. André Barbotin.
It was during that year that Mr. Barbotin was named Chef of the Year and Le Point de Vue was named Restaurant of the Year.

José is passionate about his work. His dream came true when he became the chef at a hotel in downtown Montreal and again later when he followed his career path to accept the position of chef at the Air Canada Club in the Molson Center.

Equally important, in addition to being selected as one of the top ten chefs of the decade (1990's), José Trottier has been chosen to prepare the banquet for the tenth anniversary of the Montreal Chapter of the Marmitons, an association of chefs which is renowned for its culinary achievements around the world.

Chef Trottier strives to pass on his passion for his work to his students, whom he carefully prepares for the event that they will participate in at the Grand Salon d'Art de Montreal. His pupils took the bronze medal at the most recent competition.

José is a member of the Society of Chefs, Cooks and Pastry makers of Quebec and is regularly involved as a judge in national cuisine competitions. He is also the founder of Cuisine Concept, an enterprise that attempts to establish a solid foundation of skills for participants in the areas of culinary technique, management, hygiene and healthful eating practices. Bringing healthful eating and gastronomical delights together is the mark of a great chef, José Trottier!

ÉRIC BOUTIN

Éric Boutin has been the chef at Le Paparazzi restaurant in Sillery (Quebec) for the past five years. After completing his education at Lasalle College, he began his career as the person responsible for keeping the pantries stocked at several prestigious Montreal restaurants. His enthusiasm for his job and his desire to learn at all costs served him well because when he was just 25 years old he gained his first position as a chef, which made him one of the youngest chefs in the province of Quebec.

Worthy of mention is the fact that Éric Boutin has received various honorary certificates, such as Natrel 96*, as well as two annual awards from the Quebec Pork Producers Association. Further, his ability as a communicator has led him to Radio-Canada, where he has worked as a culinary commentator for two seasons.

Also, as I am writing this book, Éric has just been chosen by the worldwide association of chefs (Les Marmitons), to receive the honorary status of guest chef, to prepare one of his gastronomical specialties for their annual banquet.

What a magnificent challenge for a chef who is only 30 years old!

* Natrel : a prominent dairy products company in Quebec.

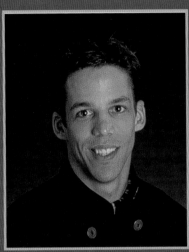

SÉBASTIEIN LEBLOND

The culinary world of Sébastien Leblond revolves around fine cuisine and the pleasures of the table. A young chef from Quebec, he grew up in an environment where cooking and catering were main components of his family life. Hard work, combined with studies in cuisine and his natural inclination to learn about the cultural traditions found around the world, led him to develop an infatuation for culinary exploration.

He likes to blend traditional methods with new culinary practices. From the fresh produce of regional growers and the creative ideas of the artisans, he combines the authentic "back to the basics" approach with "new culinary" techniques. His ongoing experimentation and his tendency to go off the beaten track, help him in his quest to find people who can transform meals into true adventures where freshness and simplicity are featured.

Sébastien Leblond also likes to pass on his knowledge of the art of good cooking. Already, he has been involved with the formation of courses in: healthful cooking; vegetarian cooking; as well as pastry making. In 1999, he was the honorary recipient of the Les Toqués award from Natrel for his presentation at a culinary competition. His particular interest in Asian cuisine, that he explores during his leisure time, has led him to carefully develop the delicious and appealing recipes that he offers to you in Tofu Gourmet Cuisine.

BENOÎT PAQUET

Son of a self-employed baker, Benoît Paquet has been immersed in gastronomical endeavours since his childhood. Twenty years ago, with his chef's diploma successfully awarded, he began his career in some of the better known Quebec establishments. As a naturally curious person he decided to travel to augment his learning, while completing training sessions in Europe and in Switzerland. Further trips to Africa and to other exotic countries gave him the opportunity to discover even more cultures and specialty dishes.

Upon his return to Quebec he was able to make his longstanding dream come true: to start his own restaurant. At that time he opened the doors of Les Copains d'abord, a restaurant that admirably presents the marvelous gastronomy of the region. All of his life and professional experiences have led him to a teaching role: it is at the Integrated Center of Food and Tourism in Quebec, where he started in 1994, that he shares his craft and his wisdom with renewed pleasure each year.

His talent and his natural curiosity have led him to take up the challenge presented to him by Frances Boyte: tofu yes, but tofu for more than just healthful eating, tofu as an exciting component of the highest form of gastronomy. What an adventure and what a great result! Tofu Gourmet Cuisine is from now on, for Benoît, one of his best legacies as a chef.

Tofu
GOURMET CUISINE

Part Two:

Rice-paper wraps with prawns and tofu

By SÉBASTIEN LEBLOND

Degree of difficulty*

Cost $$

For 4 to 8 people

Preparation: to be made ahead

Note: appetizer or main dish

MARINADE:
1 cup or 250 ml Teriyaki sauce of your choice
2 tbsp. or 30 ml ground chili paste Harissa**

INGREDIENTS:
4 giant tiger prawns peeled and deveined
10 ounces or 300 g regular firm tofu
1 finely grated carrot
2 mild peppers of various colours
2 chopped green onions
1 curled red lettuce, cut up
2 tbsp. or 30 ml fresh coriander, finely chopped
1/4 cup or 60 ml fresh basil, finely chopped
16 sheets of rice paper (8 inches)
1 tbsp. or 30 ml seaweed cut into strips

**trademark

Marinate the prawns and tofu in 1/4 cup or 60 ml of Teriyaki sauce and 1 tbsp. or 15 ml of ground chili paste for one hour.

Clean the seaweed.

Grill the prawns and tofu on the barbeque.

Cut them into strips.

Mix the seaweed, the herbs, the tofu and the shrimp in 1/2 cup or 125 ml of Teriyaki sauce and 1 tbsp. or 15 ml of ground chili paste.

Soak the rounds of rice paper in hot water for around 1 minute.

Place a rice leaf on a dampened cloth (linen).

Garnish with the preparation and roll.

Repeat with all the rice leaves.

Serve immediately with the Teriyaki sauce for dipping.

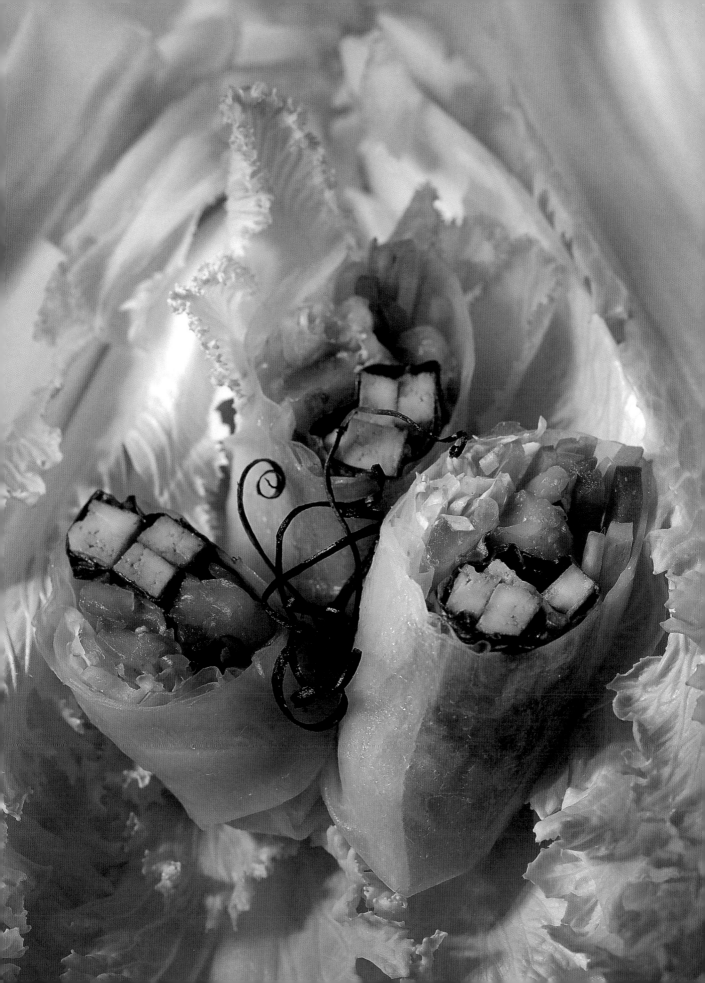

Stuffed hot avocados as found in the Andes (Columbia)

By BENOÎT PAQUET

"On a trip to Columbia, I met an elderly Lama who asked me if coca leaves could be used in this recipe! No, I answered because the dream exists in the cooking on the plate... I was joking"

Didier Girol

Degree of difficulty*
Cost $$
For 4 people
Preparation: Can be made the same day

1/4 Spanish onion finely chopped
1/2 garlic clove finely chopped
sunflower oil for cooking
150 g rice
1 1/2 cups or 375 ml poultry broth
salt and pepper to taste
6 ounces or 175 g cooked poultry breast cut into small cubes
6 ounces or 175 g firm tofu with garlic and herbs
3 ounces or 100 g grated cheddar
1 tbsp. or 15 ml coriander leaves freshly chopped
2 avocados without spots
juice of 1/2 lemon

Preheat the oven to 350 degrees F (175 degrees C).
Cook the onion and garlic in a saucepan with oil until colourless.
Add the rice and brown for 1 minute while stirring constantly.
Add the broth, salt and pepper.
Cook on a low temperature for around 15 minutes
In a bowl, mix the cooked poultry cubes, the tofu,
the coriander and half of the cheddar. Add this mixture
to the hot rice and stir together.
Cut the avocados in half and remove the pits.
Extract the pulp without damaging the skin.
Cut the pulp into small cubes and add to the rice mixture.
Moisten the avocado shells with the lemon juice.
Stuff the avocado shells with the rice mixture.
Place the avocados in a dish for the oven. Sprinkle the rest of the cheese over the avocados and cook in a hot oven until the cheese melts.
Serve hot.

Chili con tofu (Mexico)

By BENOÎT PAQUET

"For many centuries our Mexican friends have offered this vegetable based dish. I attempt to render them homage with this dish. A national treasure that can be rediscovered with tofu!"

Degree of difficulty*
Cost $
For 4 people
Preparation: Can be made in advance
Note: 12 hours of soaking (beans)

1 pound or 450 g dry kidney beans
1 pound or 450 g medium firm tofu well drained and
        chopped coarsely
corn oil for cooking
4 ounces or 120 g small cubes of beef
2 Spanish onions finely chopped
4 red tomatoes hulled, seedless and crushed
2 garlic cloves finely chopped
2 cups or 500 ml veal stock
1/2 cup or 125 ml concentrated tomato purée
4 tbsp. or 60 ml chili powder
2 bay leaves
pinch dried thyme
pinch dried oregano
pinch dried basil
salt and freshly ground pepper to taste

Soak the kidney beans in cold water in advance for 12 hours.
In a pan, brown the tofu in a small amount of oil quickly over high heat.

Add seasonings and set aside.
Brown the cubes of beef, add the onions and cook together for 2 or 3 minutes.

Add the tomatoes, veal stock, tomato purée, chili powder, bay leaves, thyme, oregano, basil, salt and pepper and cook just until the kidney beans become tender but still firm.

Add the tofu and cook again for 10 minutes.

If necessary, add some veal stock or a vegetable broth to compensate for evaporation during cooking.

Adjust the seasonings to taste and serve very hot in ramekins with nachos and melted soft cheese.

Shrimp and Shanghai tofu (China)

By BENOÎT PAQUET

Degree of difficulty*
Cost $$
For 8 people
Preparation: To be made the same day

SAUCE:
1 tsp. or 5 ml ground cumin
2 tsp. or 10 ml corn starch (or potato flour)
salt and ground white pepper to taste
1 cup or 250 ml vegetable broth
1 tbsp. or 15 ml rice wine or dry Sherry
1 tsp. or 5 ml tomato purée

1/2 pound or 250 g fresh pink peeled shrimp
7 ounces or 200 g firm tofu well drained and cut into sticks
4 egg whites lightly beaten
2 pinches of salt
2 pinches of freshly ground black pepper
sesame oil for cooking
4 ounces or 120 g frozen peas or fresh precooked
1 green onion (chives) roughly chopped
1 hot red pepper finely chopped marinated in pickling vinegar

SAUCE:
Thin the cornstarch with the wine. Mix all the dry ingredients and gradually add the liquid ingredients.
Bring to a boil while stirring constantly with a whisk.
Set aside.

Remove the dorsal veins from the shrimp and rinse in cold water.
Put the shrimp in a bowl and add the tofu, egg whites and salt and pepper.

Mix well and place in the refrigerator for 30 minutes.
In a wok or a deep pan, fry the shrimp and tofu quickly (around 2 minutes) in very warm sesame oil. Set aside.
In the wok (deep pan) sauté the peas, green onions and red pepper for 1 minute at a moderate heat.

Add the sauce and bring to a very slow boil for 2 minutes.Add the shrimp and tofu.
Serve.

You can serve this recipe over a bed of rice vermicelli cooked in boiling salted water.

Tofu falafels with cumin (Middle East)

By ÉRIC BOUTIN

Degree of difficulty*
Cost $
For 4 people
Preparation: 15 minutes
Note: Appetizer or main dish

14 ounces or 400 g canned, well drained chick peas
1/4 cup or 60 g tofu
1 cup or 250 ml olive oil
2 tbsp. or 25 g whole wheat flour
5 tbsp. or 25 g dried salted cracker crumbs (soda)
4 tsp. or 20 ml cumin powder*
1 tsp. or 5 ml salt
1/2 tsp. or 2.5 ml pepper
2 cups or 500 ml oil for frying
1 tbsp. or 15 g parsley

*cumin has a distinct flavour.
  Adjust the quantity according to your taste.

In a food processor, mix all the ingredients well, (except the oil for frying) until a firm batter is formed.

Heat oil for deep frying just until a piece of bread browns in it after 15 to 20 seconds.

Shape batter into small balls and fry the falafels until they reach a nice golden colour.

Serve as an appetizer or a main dish with a salad.

This is a good accompaniment for your salads or favourite fish.

These little fried balls will surprise and delight your guests.

Scandinavian marinated salmon and creamy tofu

By BENOÎT PAQUET

"Serve with a small glass of Aquavit. Your guests will discover that this is paradise!"

Degree of difficulty*

Cost $$

For 6 to 8 people

Note: Marinate for 24 hours

2 fillets of 1 pound or 500 g each salmon*
(taken from the thickest part of
fresh Atlantic salmon)
a small amount of olive oil for brushing
after marinating

*Preparation of the salmon: ask the person from whom you buy your fish to prepare the fillets carefully, removing the bones but leaving the skin.

MARINADE:
1 cup or 200 g cooking salt for marinating
1/2 cup or 100 g brown sugar
1/3 cup or 50 g ground black pepper
1 bay leaf crushed by hand
a pinch dried thyme
1 large bunch crushed fresh aneth (fennel),
stems and leaves

Mix all the marinade ingredients.

Place one fillet of salmon, skin side down on a layer of plastic wrap.
Brush the marinade over the fish and cover with the second fillet (flesh against flesh). Wrap very carefully (double wrap) to avoid the escape of the marinade which will partially liquefy.

Place the fillets in a deep soup bowl and put a weight of about 4 pounds or 2 kg in the bowl to press down on the salmon.

Marinate for 24 hours while turning over the packet about 3 or 4 times.

THE NEXT DAY:
Lay the fillets out and save the juice from the marinade.
Rinse the fillets under cold water and pat dry with absorbent paper.
On a cutting board, brush each fillet with olive oil and cut into thin escalopes (fillets cut diagonally into very thin slices, starting at the tail end) while taking care to regularly oil the knife (use a thin, metal, well-sharpened knife).

CREAMY TOFU:
8 ounces or 250 g creamy tofu
2 tbsps. or 45 ml 35% cream, thick or double cream
some leaves crushed fresh aneth (fennel)

Mix all together.

Place the salmon slices on the plates and cover with creamy tofu.
Decorate with the fresh aneth (fennel) leaves and slices of lime.

Quail and smoked duck consommé with silken tofu cappucino style

By MARIE-CHANTAL LEPAGE

Degree of difficulty *

Cost $$

For 4 people

QUAIL CONSOMMÉ:
1 pound or 500 g quail bones
1/2 head of garlic
1 medium carrot
1 leek
1 onion
1 bunch mixed herbs
1/4 tsp. or 1 ml whole pepper
1 clove
8 ounces or 250 g silken tofu
4 lemon zest
salt and pepper to taste

CONSOMMÉ GARNISH:
2 ounces or 50 g smoked duck cut
         julienne style
1/2 medium carrot cut julienne style
1/3 leek cut julienne style

Prehcat oven to 350 degrees F (175 degrees C).

Brown the quail bones for fifteen to twenty minutes on a baking sheet.

Transfer to a large pot and add 2 liters of cold water.

Bring to a boil and regularly skim off fat which rises to the surface. Salt.

During this time, cut the carrot, the leek and the onion pierced with the clove into large pieces.

Add the clove. Add the vegetables and the bunch of mixed herbs into the pot.
Cook covered for four hours at least at a slow boil.

Remove the quail bones and strain the broth.
Set aside.

Mix the silken tofu with the lemon zest.

Salt and pepper to taste.

Garnish each bowl with the julienne styled vegetables and the smoked duck.

Pour the consommé over each bowl.

Place the silken tofu on top and garnish with a fresh herb.

Tofu fondue with parmesan (Italy)

By BENOÎT PAQUET

"The only thing missing will be the mandolins, as you think you are in Italy. A small, romantic dish!"

Didier Girol

Degree of difficulty*
Cost $
For 4 people
Preparation: Can be made in advance
Note: Appetizer or main dish

COATING:
as needed: flour
1 beaten egg
as needed: dried bread crumbs

FONDUE BALLS:
1 pound or 500 g firm tofu well drained
7 ounces or 200 g grated parmesan cheese
2 egg whites
2 tbsp. or 30 ml freshly cut basil
pinch ground nutmeg
6 tbsp. or 90 ml corn starch (or potato flour)
salt and ground white pepper to taste

Place all ingredients in a food processor and set at speed 2 for 2 minutes or just until you have a smooth and homogeneous batter. Place the preparation in a square glass or stainless steel dish and place in the refrigerator for around 1 hour.
Once the preparation has hardened, divide into 16 equal portions and shape into small balls.
Steam the balls without stacking them for around 12 minutes. Refrigerate them for 15 minutes.
Coat the balls in flour, then in the beaten egg and roll them in dried bread crumbs. For a better result, place the balls again in the beaten egg and dried bread crumbs.
When ready to serve, place the balls in a deep fryer until golden and then immediately place them on romaine lettuce leaves accompanied by quartered tomatoes. Decorate the plate with a slice of lemon and fresh basil leaves.

Roman tofu fritos (Italy)

By BENOÎT PAQUET

"To accompany this crunchy and fragrant dish, I recommend a marvelous, young and lively Italian red wine: a Rubesco, from the cellars of Lungarotti. This wine blends delightfully with tomato dishes and…lends promise to an exciting evening!"

Degree of difficulty*
Cost $$
For 4 people
Note: A long preparation

FRITO BATTER:
1¹/3 cups or 250 g sifted flour
3 eggs
1 cup or 250 ml beer
fine salt to taste
3 egg whites in stiff peaks

SAUCE:
1/4 Spanish onion finely chopped
2 garlic cloves finely chopped
pinch oregano
pinch basil (dried)
1 bay leaf
2 tbsp. or 30 ml Italian parsley freshly chopped
1/3 cup or 100 ml white Cinzano
well ripened tomatoes, hulled, seedless and finely chopped
salt and freshly ground white pepper to taste

Place the flour in the bottom of a salad bowl and form a hollow.
In the centre, place the eggs, beer and salt and mix.
With a rubber spatula, delicately blend the flour mixture without making lumps. Blend until the batter is smooth.
Cover the batter with plastic wrap and keep in the refrigerator for one hour. When ready, beat the egg whites until stiff peaks form and add delicately to the mixture.

SAUCE:
In a deep heavy frying pan, lightly cook the onion and garlic for 2 minutes while stirring constantly to avoid browning.
Add the oregano, basil, bay leaf and the Cinzano.
Simmer the sauce to reduce the mixture to one half.
Add the tomatoes and cook for 10 minutes while stirring.
Salt and pepper and keep warm.
8 Rectangles of tofu with garlic and fine herbs:
        3¹/4 inches x 1¹/4 inches x 1/2 inch or 8 cm x 3 cm x 1 cm.
Oil for frying, Italian parsley for decoration.
Dredge the 8 rectangles of tofu in flour.
Preheat the deep fryer to 360 degrees F (180 degrees C).
Place the tofu rectangles in the frito batter and submerse in very hot oil.
When golden, drain on a clean cloth (linen).
Coat 4 heated plates with the sauce and place 2 fritos on each plate.
Sprinkle with Italian parsley and serve immediately.

Kifta lamb and tofu from the Nile Valley (Egypt)

By BENOÎT PAQUET

"When I was in Mallawi, in Egypt, I tasted this marvelous dish accompanied with sesame galettes and a wonderful yogurt made from ewe's milk. I can still taste it!"

Degree of difficulty*
Cost $$$
For 8 people
Preparation: To be made the same day

olive oil for cooking
1 spanish onion finely chopped
2 garlic cloves finely chopped
12 ounces or 400 g thinly sliced lamb
12 ounces or 400 g firm tofu well drained, cut coarsely
6 large green olives finely chopped
4 eggs
2 tbsp. or 30 ml fresh parsley cut coarsely
salt and freshly ground black pepper to taste
1 cup or 250 g Tahine (sesame paste)
1/3 cup or 100 g pine nuts

Note:
Three hours in advance, keep a small amount of olive oil in the refrigerator to congeal. This oil will be used to brush on the mold container for baking the Kifta.

Preheat the oven to 350 degrees F (175 degrees C).
In a deep thick pan, brown the onion and garlic in a small amount of olive oil.

In a salad bowl, mix all the ingredients except the tahine and pine nuts.

Brush a round hinged container (springform) with the hardened olive oil and pour in the previous mixture. Push down and smoothen the mold.

Spread the tahine evenly over the surface.
Bake for 45 minutes.
Sprinkle pine nuts on the surface and bake just until they are evenly coloured.

Stuffed peppers (Italy)

By SÉBASTIEN LEBLOND

Degree of difficulty*
Cost $$
For 6 people
Preparation: Fairly long

6 peppers
4 tbsp. or 60 ml olive oil
1 chopped onion
2 chopped garlic cloves
2 anchovy fillets chopped
3 tomatoes, hulled, seedless and cut into cubes
2 tbsp. or 30 ml cognac
1 cup or 225 g cooked basmati rice (white or brown)
1/4 cup or 60 g mozzarella cut into cubes
1/4 cup or 60 g firm tofu cut into cubes
2 tbsp. or 30 g grated grana padano or fresh parmesan
2 tbsp. or 30 g parsley
4 tsp. or 20 ml fresh basil
salt and pepper to taste
tomato sauce (optional)

Preheat the oven to 375 degrees F (190 degrees C).
Slice off the tops of the peppers and remove seeds. Blanch them in boiling salted water for 3 minutes.
Drain them on a grill, topside down.
In a pan, heat oil and brown the onion.
Add the garlic and anchovies.
Add the tomatoes and cognac.
Cook 5 minutes and remove from the burner.
Add the mixture of rice, mozzarella, tofu and one half of the grana padano.
Salt and pepper the insides of the peppers. Stuff them.
Sprinkle the rest of the grana padano.
Dribble with olive oil.
Bake in the oven for 15 to 20 minutes.
Serve immediately with tomato sauce of your choice or use the recipe for tomato sauce found on page 100.
To hull the tomatoes, make a cross in the skin and immerse in boiling water for 30 seconds. Immediately cool them and remove the skins under running cold water.

Grilled wraps of goat cheese and tofu

By ÉRIC BOUTIN

Degree of difficulty*

Cost $

For 4 people

Preparation: 20 minutes

VINAIGRETTE: (French dressing)
2 tbsp. or 30 ml olive oil
1 tsp. or 5 ml balsamic vinegar

Mix the oil and balsamic vinegar.
Set aside

WRAP INGREDIENTS:
4 large lettuce leaves (romaine or curled)
4 dried, rehydrated tomatoes,
            sliced into thin strips
4 tbsp. or 60 ml goat's cheese
4 slices of tofu, 1/2 inch x 1 inch x 1 inch
            or 1.5 cm x 2.5 cm x 2.5 cm
4 thin slices of prosciutto
4 garlic croutons in cubes
            of about 1 inch or 2.5 cm

Note:
Cut the tofu and croutons into the same size.

Place the lettuce leaves in the microwave and cook on high for around 10 seconds.

Spread the lettuce leaves out on your working table.

Place, in order and in the centre of each leaf,
the dried tomato, 1 tbsp. of goat's cheese,
1 slice of tofu and 1 slice of prosciutto.

Finish with the croutons.

Fold the leaves into a wrap and grill on the barbeque,
or place in a very hot oven for a few minutes.

Pour the vinaigrette on the bottom of each plate to be served.

Place the wraps on the balsamic vinegar and olive oil.

Add a thin pancake, shaped as in the picture and dried in a microwave oven.

Serve.

West Indian crêpes with tofu and seafood

By BENOÎT PAQUET

"Imagine coconut palm trees bending towards the sea. A soft sea wind caresses you and the punch glasses are clinking together. All right, I will stop. Here it is cold and it snows."

Didier Girol

Degree of difficulty*

Cost $$$

For 4 people

Note: Prepare the crêpes

olive oil for cooking
3 small grey shallots chopped finely
1 clove of garlic chopped finely
1/2 green pepper cut in small cubes
1/2 red pepper cut in small cubes
3 tomatoes, hulled, seedless and crushed
4 ounces or 120 g cooked, peeled pink shrimp
4 ounces or 120 g small freshly cooked scallops
4 ounces or 120 g cooked mussels, unshelled
4 ounces or 120 g firm tofu, well drained
    and cut into small cubes
salt and freshly ground pepper to taste
2 tbsp. or 30 ml West Indian rum
1/2 cup or 125 ml 35% cream,
    thick or double cream
1 cup or 150 g grated cheese

SEAFOOD MIXTURE:

In a deep heavy pan, heat the oil and cook the shallots and garlic until colourless.

Add the peppers and tomatoes. Simmer uncovered for 10 minutes.

Add the shrimp, scallops, mussels and the tofu and cook 2 minutes.

Salt, pepper and add the rum

Set oven temperature to "grill"

CRÊPES:
Fill each crêpe with seafood mixture and shape them (roll up).

Arrange on a cheese topped dish and pour cream over all.

Sprinkle with grated cheese.

When ready to serve, place in the oven until the cheese is golden.

Breaded tofu with dried tomato pesto (Italy)

By ÉRIC BOUTIN

Mix all the pesto ingredients in a blender until the mixture is smooth.

Set aside.

Mix the egg and the milk. Dip the slices of tofu in the flour and then in the egg and milk mixture.

Dip in the cracker crumbs.

In a small amount of oil, fry the tofu on a high heat until a nice colour.

Pour the dried tomato pesto over the tofu slices and garnish with fresh basil.

Degree of difficulty*
Cost $$$
For 4 people
Preparation: 15 minutes

PESTO:
4 tsp. or 20 ml dried, rehydrated tomatoes
1 tsp. or 4 g pine nuts
1/2 tsp. or 2.5 ml crushed garlic
4 tbsp. or 60 ml extra virgin olive oil
2 tbsp. or 30 ml parmesan (Grana Padano)
12 fresh basil leaves

COATING:
1 egg
1/3 cup or 100 ml milk
4 slices of tofu, 1 1/4 inches or 3 cm in diameter
1/3 cup or 100 g unbleached white flour
1/3 cup or 100 g dry salted cracker crumbs

Warm tofu salad with duck liver and raspberry vinegar (International)

By BENOÎT PAQUET

"An intimate little supper, under the arbour in September? This is the ideal dish. Accompanied by a fresh little rosé from Provence, the only thing that will be missing will be the violins!"
Didier Girol

Degree of difficulty*
Cost $$
For 4 people
Preparation:
to be made same day

SAUCE:
sunflower oil for cooking
1 large chopped shallot
3/4 cup or 200 ml raspberry vinegar
10 peppercorns
a pinch dried thyme
1 bay leaf
1 garlic clove
1 1/2 cups or 375 ml brown veal stock
1/2 cup or 125 ml 35% cream, thick or double cream
salt and freshly ground white pepper to taste
sugar to taste

GARNITURE:
mixed baby greens or romaine lettuce to taste
6 ounces or 200 g fresh, deveined duck liver*
6 ounces or 200 g white regular tofu cut into sticks of
      1/2 inch x 2 1/2 inches or 1.25 cm x 6 cm
salt and freshly ground pepper
sunflower oil for cooking

*Grain fed duck

SAUCE:
In a saucepan, cook shallots gradually in a small amount of sunflower oil until golden.
Add the raspberry vinegar, pepper, thyme, bay leaf and the garlic clove. Cook until you are left with 1 tbsp. or 15 ml of liquid.
Add the stock and simmer on a low heat uncovered for 20 to 30 minutes.
Add the cream and cook 2 to 3 minutes without bringing to a boil.
Strain the sauce through a sieve.
Balance the acidity with the addition of sugar.
Salt and pepper and keep warm.

GARNITURE:
Place a bed of lettuce on 4 plates.
Salt and pepper the liver and tofu.
In a non stick pan, coated with a small amount of sunflower oil, fry the liver and tofu quickly on a brisk heat. The liver must be pink inside.
Divide and arrange the liver and tofu on the beds of lettuce.
Coat with warm sauce.

Spanakopita with tofu (Middle East)

By JOSÉ TROTTIER

"Ask your children to help you arrange the spanakopitas. They will definitely appreciate it!"

Degree of difficulty**
Cost $
For 4 people
Preparation: Long, a little family project
Note: Appetizers (canapés) or main dish

2 pounds or 1 kg spinach
olive oil for cooking
1 cup or 250 ml chopped onions
1/3 cup or 85 ml well drained feta cheese
1/3 cup or 85 ml well drained cottage cheese
3 tbsp. or 45 ml parmesan
1/3 cup or 85 ml well drained firm tofu
1 pinch nutmeg
sea salt and white pepper to taste
3 eggs
1 package filo pastry

FOR A MAIN DISH:
Preheat the oven to 375 degrees F (190 degreesC).
Clean the spinach and remove the central rib from each leaf.
Place the spinach in a pot of boiling water for 1 minute to soften.
Remove the spinach and run under cold water to stop cooking.
Drain the spinach well.
Set aside in a mixing bowl.
Fry the onions lightly in 2 tbsp. of olive oil.
Add the spinach, cheeses, tofu, nutmeg, salt and pepper
to the onions. Mix well.
Beat the eggs and add to the mixture.
Oil a large, slightly deep dish for the oven.
Brush some oil on 12 sheets of filo pastry.
Cover the bottom of the dish with 6 sheets of pastry.
Spread the filling evenly over the pastry.
Cover with the remaining 6 sheets of pastry.
Bake in the oven for 40 to 50 minutes until the crust is golden.

FOR AN APPETIZER OR CANAPÉS:
Preheat the oven to 375 degrees F (190 degrees C).
Brush oil on a sheet of filo pastry.
Cut the sheet of filo pastry into 3 strips lengthwise.
Place one tablespoon of the mixture in the
bottom corner of each strip.
Fold into a triangle above the filling.
Continue to fold the triangle for the length of the strip.
Place in the oven for 15 to 20 minutes.

Tofu and curry dip (Canada)

By LINE DÉSILETS

"Life has given me a wonderful gift: HEALTH, but I must work hard to maintain it. Healthy nutrition helps me to preserve this health and helps me obtain peace and happiness!"

Degree of difficulty*
Cost $
For one cup of dip

6 ounces or 180 g tofu
1 1/2 tbsp. or 45 ml lemon juice
2 tbsp. or 30 ml oil (olive, sunflower or sesame)
1/4 tsp. or 1.25 ml salt
1 tsp. or 5 ml tamari
2 tbsp. or 30 ml chopped onion
1/2 tsp. or 2.5 ml curry powder
1 tbsp. or 15 ml parsley

Mix all the ingredients in an electric mixer. Add a small amount of water if the consistency is too thick.

VARIATION:
With a little more oil, you will have an excellent vinegarette.
(French dressing)

Sushi with nectarines and smoked salmon

By ÉRIC BOUTIN

*"This dish is a variation of classical sushi without rice.
However, if you prefer the taste of rice… don't be shy, use it!"*

Degree of difficulty*

Cost $$

For 4 people

Preparation: 15 to 30 minutes

SAUCE:
1/2 cup or 125 ml orange juice
2 tsp. or 10 ml sesame oil
3 tsp. or 15 ml soya sauce

SUSHI:
1 cup or 250 ml orange juice
10 ounces or 300 ml thinly sliced
    smoked salmon
1/4 cup or 60 g cucumber flesh cut into sticks
1 ounce or 30 g Brie cut into sticks
1$^{1}/_{3}$ ounces or 40 g regular firm tofu
    cut into sticks
3 ounces or 90 g nectarines cut into sticks
4 nori leaves (green seaweed)
Wasabi* to taste

*Wasabi: very strong Japanese horseradish

Mix the sauce ingredients and set aside.

Using a brush, cover the dull side of the nori leaves with orange juice.

Place the slices of smoked salmon on the leaves, covering as much as possible.

At around 1 inch or 2.5 cm from the border, spread the sticks of brie, tofu and nectarines in a straight line.

Roll into a cylinder and slice into rounds with a very hot, wet knife

Serve with Wasabi.

WINE SUGGESTION: Entre-Deux-Mers or Sake

Crispy tofu with mushrooms, Roquefort sauce and basil

By BENOÎT PAQUET

Degree of difficulty*

Cost $$

For 4 people

Preparation:
Can be made the day before

Note: Appetizer or main dish

INGREDIENTS No. 1
2 ounces or 60 g shallots*
1 cup or 250 ml dry white wine
1 bay leaf
a pinch dried thyme
20 grains black pepper
4 juniper berries

INGREDIENTS No. 2
1 cup or 250 ml brown veal stock

BUTTER THICKENER
2 tbsp. or 30 g creamed butter with 2 tbsp.
            or 30 g of flour

INGREDIENTS No. 3
3 ounces or 100 g Roquefort
1/2 cup or 125 ml 35% cream,
            thick or double cream
salt and white pepper to taste
freshly cut basil to taste

*shallots: often called french or grey shallots.
Note: set aside some pieces of Roquefort and
basil leaves for decoration.

In a saucepan, gently bring all the ingredients in No.1 to a boil.
Cook lightly until you have about 1/2 cup or 125 ml of juice.
Add the veal stock and bring back to a boil.
Blend in the butter mixture with a whisk (removed from the burner).
Return to the burner and simmer on a low heat for 20 minutes.
Strain the sauce through a cheese cloth.
Bring the strained sauce back to a boil and add No.3
ingredients while stirring constantly until the cheese
is thoroughly melted. Set aside.

CRUST:
4 sheets filo pastry
sunflower oil for cooking

Preheat the oven to 400 degrees F (200C).
On a chopping board, stack 4 sheets of filo pastry first brushed
with sunflower oil.
Using a cutter, prepare 4 circles of 4 inches or 10 cm in diameter.
Place the rounds on a cookie sheet and cook in the oven for a
few minutes until golden in colour.
Note: These can be kept many days when cooled in an
airtight container.

GARNISH: WHEN READY TO SERVE
olive oil for cooking
8 ounces or 225 g cultivated mushrooms cut in quarters
20 ounces or 600 g firm tofu cut into 3/4 inch cubes or 2 cm
salt and freshly ground pepper to taste
4 tbsp. or 60 ml aniseed alcohol (Ricard, Pastis, etc.)

In a deep pan with a small amount of oil brown the mushrooms
over a brisk heat.
When the mushrooms are golden, add the cubes of tofu
and continue cooking over a brisk heat for 2 minutes.
Salt and pepper.
Flambé with the aniseed alcohol and immediately pour the
Roquefort sauce into the pan to extinguish the flame.

ATTENTION: ALWAYS FLAMBÉ WITHOUT BEING NEAR THE STOVE.
For serving, divide the final preparation on to 4 heated plates.
Place a crust on each garnish. Decorate with small pieces of
Roquefort and fresh basil leaves.

Saltimbanque of grilled vegetables and tofu (Italy)

By SÉBASTIEN LEBLOND

"Great in the autumn with the garden harvest."

Degree of difficulty*
Cost $$
For 4 people
Recommendation: Ideal for the barbeque

MARINADE:
1 cup or 250 ml orange juice
3/4 cup or 200 ml olive oil
3 tbsp. or 45 ml balsamic vinegar
3 tbsp. or 45 ml strong mustard
2 chopped garlic cloves

VINEGARETTE (FRENCH DRESSING)
1/2 cup or 125 ml olive oil
3 tbsp. or 45 ml balsamic vinegar
1 medium unpeeled eggplant cut into
          8 slices of 1/4 inch or 1/2 cm
1 scrubbed portabella mushroom cut into slices
2 squash (zucchini) cut into strips
1 sliced red onion
2 red peppers cut into thin round slices
6 ounces or 180 g tofu in strips
4 ounces or 120 g goat's cheese
12 basil leaves

Preheat the barbeque to a high heat and the oven to 350 degrees F (175 degreesC).
Marinate the vegetables and tofu for 30 to 60 minutes.
Grill all the vegetables and tofu on the barbeque.

Next, on a lightly oiled baking tray, stack 1 round of eggplant, one slice of mushroom, 1 strip of zucchini, 1 slice of onion, 1 round of pepper, 1 strip of tofu and 1 round of goat's cheese.

Repeat this function again to obtain one Saltimbanque*

Cook in the oven for 10 minutes.

Place one Saltimbanque in the centre of each plate then moisten with the vinegarette and garnish with basil leaves.

*Saltimbanque: a cooking term used in cooking to express "by layers or stuffing".

Tofu and shrimp with sweet cream corn

(Huron-Wenndatt, Quebec)

By BENOÎT PAQUET

"We have an image that the American Indians eat only buffalo and beaver. Well, this recipe proves it is not true!"

Didier Girol

Degree of difficulty*
Cost $$
For 4 people
Preparation: To be made the same day

3 cobs sweet fresh corn
1/2 cup or 125 ml 35% cream, thick or double cream
salt and ground white pepper to taste
16 slices tofu with fine herbs
12 large peeled pink shrimp
corn oil for cooking
juice of 1/2 lemon
20 sweet peas (for the garnish)
1/2 tomato cut in small cubes (for the garnish)

Remove the kernels from the cobs with a small knife. Process the kernels through a juice extractor.
In a deep heavy pan, reduce the juice from the corn to one half over a slow heat.
Add the cream and cook over a slow heat for 5 minutes.
Season and set aside.
Place the slices of tofu (16 slices of 2.5 inches x 1 inch or 6 cm x 2.5 cm approximately) on a cookie sheet.
Salt and pepper each slice. Set the oven to "grill".

Cook the slices of tofu until golden and set aside.
When ready to serve: sauté the shrimp seasoned with salt and pepper in a non stick pan with a small amount of corn oil.
Reheat the sauce and tofu.

Place 4 slices of tofu on each plate. Cover with sauce.
Arrange the shrimp on the plates and decorate with sugar peas cooked, but crunchy, and the tomato cubes.
Serve with bannock (recipe on page 106).

Avocado soup with tofu (Mexico)

(sopa de aguacate con tofu)

By BENOÎT PAQUET

"A lovely presentation for a summer evening on the terrace."

Degree of difficulty*
Cost $$
For 8 people
Preparation : To be made the same day

3 well ripened avocados
1/2 cup or 125 ml creamy tofu
1/2 cup or 125 ml 35% cream, thick or double cream
6 cups or 1.5 litres poultry or vegetable broth
8 tbsps. or 120 ml sherry
Salt and ground white pepper to taste

Note : GARNISH
Prepare some strips of tortillas, some thin slices of avocado and some small cubes of firm tofu.
Sprinkle with fresh coriander and set aside.

Peel the avocados and cut them in half, remove the pit. Reduced the flesh to a purée.

Add the creamy tofu and the cream bit by bit to the purée. Mix well and set aside.

Heat the broth on a high heat in a stainless steel pot.

When the broth is boiling, add the avocado mixture by spoonfuls while mixing well with a whisk.

Add the sherry. Salt and pepper to taste.

Pour the soup into a tureen and serve with the garnish of tortillas, avocado and tofu.

Each guest will be able to select his own garnish.
In the summer, this soup can be served cold.
It is excellent and very refreshing.

For the cold mixture, place them on shredded lettuce.

Bali soup (Indonesia)

By GILLES PARENT

"To make this dish into a meal, serve this soup over brown basmati rice. An excellent, quick meal!"

Degree of difficulty*
Cost $
For 6 people

10 green onions finely chopped
14 ounces or 420 ml coconut milk
3 to 4 tbsp. or 45 to 60 ml tamari sauce
2 tsp. or 10 ml brown sugar
1 1/2 tsp. or 7.5 ml curry
1 tsp. or 5 ml fresh ginger
1 to 2 tsp. or 5 to 10 ml garlic chili paste
12 ounces of tofu regular or silken
4 tomatoes (preferably Italian) cut into 6 pieces
1 yellow pepper thinly sliced
1/4 pound or 125 g sliced mushrooms
          (preferably shiitake)
1/4 cup or 65 ml Freshly cut basil
4 cups or 1 litre bok choy (green part only) or spinach
salt and pepper to taste

Cut the green onions finely (the white part only and set aside the green part for decoration). In a thick, deep pan, mix the coconut milk, tamari sauce, brown sugar, curry, ginger and the chili paste. Gradually bring to the boiling point.
Add the tofu, tomatoes, yellow pepper, mushrooms, basil and the green onions.

Cover and cook 5 minutes. Stir occasionally.

Add the bok choy and cover and cook again for 5 minutes or just until the vegetables are *al dente*. Stir occasionally.
Salt and pepper to taste. Adjust the seasonings to taste.
Garnish with the reserved green onions.

Gilles Parent is a born commentator. He started at the microphone at seventeen years of age and he just turned forty; always in top form on his comedy show, La Jungle, which has been the most popular comedy show in the history of Quebec radio since it began in 1985. Also, three years ago, he and his three brothers launched the site, Internet Showbizz.net (www.showbizz.net). Gilles Parent is a well known person who is always in the public eye in the field of communications in Quebec. He is known for his vision, his leadership and his winning ways.

Anise flavoured small shrimp with tofu (Canada)

By BENOÎT PAQUET

"This dish is fresh, tasty and intoxicating!"

Degree of difficulty*
Cost $$
For 4 people
Preparation : Can be made the day before

INGREDIENTS No. 1
olive oil for cooking
3 tbsp. or 45 ml chopped onion
2 tbsp. or 30 ml thinly sliced white of leek
2 tbsp. or 30 ml chopped celery
2 tbsp. or 30 ml small carrot cubes
4 cups or 1 litre fish broth
1 bay leaf
a pinch dried thyme
1/2 crushed garlic clove
2 tbsp. or 30 ml concentrated tomato purée

INGREDIENTS No. 2
150 g small peeled shrimp
1/4 cup or 40 g uncooked white rice

INGREDIENTS No. 3
150 g firm tofu well drained and cut into small cubes
3 tbsp. or 45 ml 35% cream, thick or double cream
sea salt and freshly ground white pepper to taste
        (or a pinch of cayenne)

GARNITURE:
1 tbsp. or 15 ml finely sliced chives
some drops anise flavoured liquor

Cook all the vegetables in No. 1 in a small amount of olive oil in a covered pot over a low heat for about 2 minutes.

Add the fish broth and the rest of the ingredients in No. 1 (garlic, bay leaf, thyme, tomato purée). Cover and simmer over a low heat for about 10 minutes.

Strain the broth.

Bring the broth to a boil.

Add the No. 2 ingredients.
Cover and simmer over a low heat for 15 minutes.

Pour the mixture into a strainer to regain the rice and shrimp. Set aside some shrimp for the decoration. Place the rice and shrimp in a grinder (medium grind).

Mix the rice and shrimp purée with the broth and bring to a boil.

Add the tofu and cream. At the first signs of boiling, it is ready. Season to taste.

When ready to serve, place a few shrimp, a pinch of chives and a few drops of anise flavoured liquor in each bowl.

Tomato soup with tofu (Quebec)

By GINETTE FLEURY

"After having experienced really intense stress, she discovered the importance of food and supplements for her serenity!"

Frances Boyte

Degree of difficulty*
Cost $
For 4 people

1 tbsp. or 15 ml olive oil
1 chopped onion
1 tbsp. or 15 ml all purpose flour
28 ounces or 750 ml fresh Italian tomatoes cut into cubes
2¹/₂ cups or 625 ml vegetable broth
     (set aside 1/2 cup or 125 ml)
1 tsp. or 5 ml dried oregano
1/4 tsp. or 1.25 ml black pepper
salt to taste
8 ounces or 250 g soft tofu
1 tbsp. or 15 ml honey
1 tbsp. or 15 ml dried aneth (fennel)

Brown the onion in the olive oil. Add the flour and cook for 1 minute.

Add the tomatoes, 2 cups of vegetable broth, oregano and salt and pepper.

Set aside.

In a mixer, add the tofu, the reserved broth (1/2 cup) as well as the honey and reduce all to a purée.

Add the tofu mixture and aneth (fennel) to the tomato mixture and simmer about 5 minutes.

VARIATION :
Replace the oregano and aneth with fresh basil that you would add in the last five minutes of cooking.

Saint-Germain soup with smoked tofu (France)

By BENOÎT PAQUET

Degree of difficulty*
Cost $
For 4 people
Preparation : Can be made the day before

sunflower oil for cooking
1 cup or 100 g chopped Spanish onion
1/2 cup or 50 g chopped white of leek
1 cup or 300 g green split peas
1 bay leaf
a pinch dried thyme
8 cups or 2 litres poultry or vegetable broth
1/2 carrot
salt and freshly ground pepper to taste
1/2 cup or 125 ml 35% cream
garlic fried croutons
10 ounces or 300 g smoked tofu cut into small cubes*

*Smoked tofu can be found in speciality stores.

Put a small amount of oil in a covered saucepan and cook the onions and leeks on a low heat for about 2 minutes until moisture appears.

Add the peas, bay leaf, thyme, broth, carrot and salt and pepper. Bring slowly to a boil and simmer gently until the split peas are cooked (about 45 minutes to 1 hour and 15 minutes). Under the pressure of your fingers, the peas must be reduced to a purée. Remove the bay leaf and carrot.

Place the mixture in a blender and blend just until it has a smooth homogeneous texture.

Pour the soup into a pot and bring to a boil.
Add the cream while stirring.

When the boiling resumes, stop the cooking and adjust seasonings to your taste. Set aside to cool.
When ready to serve, reheat the soup, pour into bowls and garnish with the croutons and smoked tofu.
Sprinkle lightly with paprika.

Scottish soup with tofu (Scotland)

By JOSÉ TROTTIER

" This substantial soup shows the vigour of these people"

Degree of difficulty*
Cost $
For 4 people

2 tbsp. or 30 ml safflower oil
1 carrot cut into cubes
1 stick of celery cut into cubes
1 red onion cut into cubes
1 red potato cut into cubes
1/4 tsp. or 1.25 ml thyme
1 pinch rosemary
3 cups or 750 ml chicken broth
1/4 cup or 65 ml frozen green peas
1/2 pound or 750 g tofu in brine*, cubed
1/2 cup or 125 ml 35% cream, thick or double cream
sea salt and white pepper to taste
1 tbsp. or 15 ml chervil

*Tofu in brine is sold in grocery stores specializing in
 Chinese food products and in some supermarkets.

Brown the carrot, the celery and onion in oil.

Add the potato, herbs and broth.

Cook just until the vegetables are tender.

Add the tofu and cream.

Heat without allowing mixture to boil.

Adjust the seasonings to taste and add the chervil
when ready to serve.

Gaspacho (Spain)

By BENOÎT PAQUET

"A simple and refreshing little recipe for the summer. A pre-taste of the holidays!"

Degree of difficulty*
Cost $
For 16 people
Preparation : Can be made in advance

4 pounds or 2 kg ripe tomatoes, hulled,
         seedless and finely crushed
2 red peppers cut into small cubes
2 green peppers cut into small cubes
3 English cucumbers, peeled, seedless and
         cut into small cubes
1 Spanish onion chopped finely
4 garlic cloves finely chopped
4 cups or 1 litre poultry or vegetable broth
3 tbsp. + 1 tsp. olive oil
3 tbsp. or 45ml wine vinegar
3 tbsp. or 45ml sugar
3 tbsp. or 30ml mild paprika
2 tbsp. or 30ml ground cumin
salt and pepper to taste
2 ounces or 60 g / 1 portion firm tofu, well drained and
         cut into small cubes
fresh basil for decorating

Place all ingredients in a jar (earthenware) and mix well.

Refrigerate at least 1 hour before serving.

When ready to serve, place 2 ounces or 60g of the tofu cubes
(firm and well drained) on each plate.

Decorate with basil leaves.
This will easily keep for 1 week in the refrigerator.

Japanese soup

By SYLVIE BLACKBURN

Degree of difficulty*

Cost $

For 4 people

5 to 6 green onions
5 cups or 1.25 litres water
1 ounce dried Shiitake* mushrooms
        (or around 12 fresh)
1 fresh slice of ginger with skin, 1^1/$_2$ inches
        or 4 cm cut coarsely
1/4 cup or 65 ml rice miso
12 ounces or 360 g firm tofu, rinsed and
        cut into cubes of 1/2 inch or 1 cm
1 tsp. or 15 ml dry sherry
4 cups or 1 litre freshly washed spinach,
        well drained and cut
Tamari to taste

*Shiitake: The stems of the shiitake must be removed before cooking. If they are dried, remove the stems once they are moisturized.

Chop 2 green onions finely and set aside.

Put the water, mushrooms, ginger and green onions in a pot.

Cover and bring to a boil. Cook for 10 minutes.

With a skimmer (slotted spoon), withdraw the mushrooms. Let simmer for 10 minutes more.

Strain the broth and set aside.

In a bowl, whip the miso with 1 cup or 250 ml of the broth.

Place the strained broth in a pot and add the tofu and sherry and bring to a boil.

Add the mushrooms and the spinach and simmer just until the spinach is cooked.

Remove the soup from the burner and whip in the miso and tamari.

Garnish with the reserved green onions.

Serve immediately.

Sylvie Blackburn.
Her interest in life: that children are well nourished, and promoting NSA Juice Plus helps her accomplish that goal.

Spicy soup with tofu (Thailand)

By SÉBASTIEN LEBLOND

Degree of difficulty*
Cost $$
For 6 people
Preparation : To be made the same day

4 cups or 1 litre chicken broth
1 cup or 250 ml sliced mushrooms
4 ounces or 120 g clams
1/2 cup or 125 ml firm tofu cut into cubes
1/2 cup or 125 ml small shrimp
          (size 125 to 150 per pound or 500 g)
1 tbsp. or 15 ml corn starch
1 tbsp. or 15 ml raspberry vinegar
1/2 tsp. or 2.5 ml crushed pimento
2 egg whites
2 green onions

Bring the chicken broth to a boil.

Add the mushrooms, clams, tofu and the shrimp to the broth.

Dilute the cornstarch in the raspberry vinegar and add a small amount of the broth mixture. Pour into the main broth mixture to thicken.

Season to taste.

Add the crushed pimento and blend in the well beaten egg whites so that swirls are formed.

Garnish with green onion. Adjust the seasonings to taste.

Serve.

Quick tofu and ginger soup (Quebec)

By LOUISE LAMBERT-LAGACÉ

"Intriguing, subtle, irresistible, to serve for a special evening!"

Degree of difficulty*
Cost $
For 4 people
Preparation: Quick

3 cups or 750 ml poultry stock or chicken broth
3 crushed garlic cloves
16 ounces or 450 g silken extra firm tofu
          cut into cubes of 1/2 inch or 1 cm
4 tbsp. or 60 ml finely chopped onion
4 tbsp. or 60 ml freshly grated ginger
2 tbsp. or 30 ml sugar
juice of 1 lime
juice of 1/2 orange
1/2 cup or 125 ml finely chopped green onion

In a large pot, heat the poultry stock or chicken broth just until it simmers.

Add all the ingredients except the green onions.

Cook 10 minutes. Remove from the burner.

Add the green onions and serve immediately.

Author of many best-sellers on nutrition, Louise runs her nutrition clinic in Montreal and is interested in everything concerning the influence of foods on the health of humans.

Oriental soup (China)

By KERRY and MICKEY DAIGLE

Degree of difficulty*
Cost $
For 4 people
Note: Marinate 4 hours

3 1/2 ounces or 100 g silken tofu in cubes
        of 1/2 inch or 1 cm
2 large crushed garlic cloves
1/4 cup or 60 ml tamari sauce
4 finely chopped green shallots
2 tsp. or 10 ml sesame oil
6 cups or 1.5 litres chicken broth
1/2 tsp. or 2.5 ml finely chopped fresh ginger
1/4 tsp. or 1.25 ml ground cayenne pepper
1 cup or 250 ml freshly prepared spinach
10 slices mushrooms
16 peeled shrimp
pepper to taste

Marinate the tofu and garlic for at least 4 hours in the tamari sauce in the refrigerator.

Drain the tofu and save 2 tsp. or 30 ml of the marinade.

Brown the shallots in oil, add the broth and ginger. Bring to a boil.

Add the drained tofu, the reserved marinade, cayenne pepper, spinach, mushrooms, shrimp and pepper.
Simmer for 3 minutes until the shrimp are cooked and serve.

Kerry and Mickey Daigle are cajun cooks! They live in Opelousas in Louisiana. They are both authors, lecturers, and national directors of the marketing section of the Juice Plus company.

Pumpkin Velouté with tofu
(American-Indian, Canada)

By JOSÉ TROTTIER

"Pumpkin is often used in American-Indian cuisine and unrecognized in other cuisines. It is a mild, subtle, versatile food that goes well with tofu."

Degree of difficulty*
Cost $
For 4 people

2 tbsp. or 30 ml sunflower oil
1/2 cup or 125 ml thinly sliced white of leek
4 cups or 1 litre vegetable broth
1 cup or 250 ml pumpkin cut into cubes
1 tbsp. or 15 ml garlic
1 tsp. or 5 ml grated ginger
1/2 cup or 125 ml silken tofu
sea salt and white pepper to taste
1 tbsp. chervil

Brown the leeks in oil.

Add the broth and the pumpkin.

Bring to a boil and simmer 30 minutes.

Add garlic, ginger and the tofu. Simmer 15 minutes.

Mix in a blender.

Adjust seasonings to taste, add the chervil and serve.

Fish Veloute with almonds (North American)

By BENOÎT PAQUET

"A little hard to read as a recipe but very easy to make. It is worth it, trust me."

Degree of difficulty*
Cost $$
For 6 to 8 people
Preparation: Can be made the day before

VELOUTÉ:

PREPARATION No. 1
1/3 cup or 80 g butter
1 cup or 100 g chopped onions
1/2 crushed garlic clove
1 thinly sliced white of leek
1/2 stick of chopped celery
1/2 cup or 80 g flour
8 cups or 2 litres fish broth
1 cup or 250 ml white wine
100 g slivered almonds
dried thyme to taste
bay leaf to taste
a few grains black pepper

PREPARATION No. 2
1/3 cup or 100 ml 35% cream, thick or double cream
3 ounces or 100 g wall-eyed pike cut into cubes
3 ounces or 100 g halibut or sole cut into strips
3 ounces or 100 g salmon or trout fillets cut into cubes
salt and white pepper to taste

PREPARATION No. 1
Brown the onion, garlic, leek and celery in the butter for
2 minutes, add the flour and mix well.
Add, while stirring, the fish broth and white wine.
Add the almonds and cook gently for 10 minutes.
Place these ingredients in a mixer and then through a strainer.
Bring gently to a boil again.

PREPARATION No 2
Add cream to Preparation No.1 and bring to a boil.
Salt and pepper.
Add the fish and cook 3 to 4 minutes while stirring gently.
Set aside and keep warm.

NEXT ADD:
1 tomato cut into small cubes
8 ounces or 225 tsp. thinly sliced cultivated mushrooms
4 ounces or 120 tsp. fresh green beans cut into cubes
6 ounces or 180 tsp. firm tofu well drained and cut into cubes
Grilled slivered almonds for decoration
Adjust seasonings to taste.

When ready to serve, place some grilled, slivered almonds and
a small amount of chopped parsley onto the soup plates.
Pour in the velouté and serve immediately.

Soup made with soymilk, tofu, wild rice and ginger root! (Quebec)

By MARIE-CHANTAL LEPAGE

"A great soup for afternoon winter sports." - Frances Boyte

Degree of difficulty*
Cost $
For 4 people
Preparation: 20 minutes

1 cup or 250 ml regular firm tofu cut into cubes
1 cup or 250 ml whites of leeks thinly sliced
1 cup or 250 ml diced carrots
1 garlic clove minced
ginger root to taste
1 cup or 250 ml white beans
1 cup or 250 ml kidney beans
1 cup or 250 ml black beans
4 cups or 1 litre poultry stock
4 cups or 1 litre soymilk
1 cup or 250 ml wild rice
4 tbsp.or 60 ml sunflower oil
salt and pepper to taste

Cook the wild rice in boiling salted water and reserve.

Brown the carrots, the whites of the leeks in sunflower oil.

Moisten the carrots and whites of leeks with the poultry stock and
soymilk. Add garlic, ginger root, the three types of beans and tofu.

Simmer for 4 minutes and add the wild rice.

Salt and pepper.

*This soup was created by Marie-Chantal Lepage, executive chef of the
Manoir Montmorency, for an organic culinary demonstration at Metro
Gagnon Supermarkets, Quebec, Canada.*

The Salads

Tofu salad (Quebec)

By ZHOU BENDING

Degree of difficulty*
Cost $
For 4 people

8 ounces or 250 g tofu
water for cooking the tofu and green peas
2 ounces or 50 g cooked chicken breast
1 ounce or 25 g ham
1 apple
1/4 cup or 50 g green peas
2 tbsp. or 50 g mayonnaise
2 tsp. or 5 g powdered milk
2 ounces or 50 g shrimp
salt and pepper to taste

Cut the tofu into squares of 1/2 inch or 1.5cm. Place the tofu in a pan, cover with water and bring just to the boiling point. Let simmer for 5 minutes.

Rinse under cold water and drain.
Set aside.

Cut the chicken, ham and the apple into small cubes. Set aside.

Cook the green peas in boiling salted water. Drain and set aside. In a small bowl, mix the mayonnaise and the powdered milk.

Place the tofu, chicken, apple, ham, shrimp and peas in a salad bowl.

Mix with the mayonnaise and adjust seasonings to taste. Serve.

Zhou Bending is a doctor of acupuncture and a native of Beijing. He has worked in Quebec for many years. With his savoir-faire and his generosity, he works to keep the people of Quebec healthy.

Exotic seafood with fresh tempura salad (International)

By ÉRIC BOUTIN

Degree of difficulty*
Cost $$
For 4 people
Preparation: 30 minutes
Note: 6 hours of soaking

VINAIGRETTE:
5 tbsp. or 75 ml extra virgin olive oil
3 tbsp. or 45 ml mango nectar
5 tsp. or 25 ml cider or rice vinegar

1 or 140 g mango cut into cubes
1/2 cup or 100 g papaya cut into cubes
1/4 cup or 60 g avocado cut into cubes
5 tbsp. or 75 g red pepper cut into cubes
5 tbsp. or 75 g yellow pepper cut into cubes
3 tbsp. or 45 g green pepper cut into cubes
1/2 cup or 125 ml flesh of cucumber cut into cubes
2 tbsp. or 30 g chopped onion
1 chopped garlic clove
1/3 cup or 125 ml nordic shrimp cooked and cooled
1/3 cup or 125 ml small scallops
1/3 cup or 125 ml tofu cut into small cubes

Mix all the ingredients well and let soak together in the refrigerator for not less than 6 hours.

TEMPURA (BATTER):
1/2 cup or 100 g flour
1/2 cup or 125 ml milk
4 tbsp. or 60 ml baking powder
1/2 to 1 tsp. or 2 to 5 ml curry (to taste)
5 tsp. or 25 ml fruit juice (orange – grapefruit)
1 tsp. or 5 ml ground turmeric
1 large egg
2 cups or 500 ml oil for frying

Mix all the tempura ingredients together.

In two cups or 500 ml of hot oil, drop the batter in by droplets with the help of a fork to obtain small fried balls.

Serve the seafood salad on a small bed of lettuce and garnish with the small fried tempura balls.....it is delicious!

Latin American tofu salad (South America)

By JOSÉ TROTTIER

"A quick salad, with vivid colours and lots of taste!"

Degree of difficulty*
Cost $
For 4 people
Preparation: To be made the day before
Note: Appetizer or main dish

1 cup or 250 ml firm tofu
1 cup or 250 ml cooked kidney beans
1 cup or 250 ml thawed corn kernels
1 red pepper cut into cubes
1 green pepper cut into cubes

VINAIGRETTE:
1/4 cup or 65 ml corn oil
2 tbsp. or 30 ml Tamari, Shoyu
1 tbsp. or 15 ml lime juice
1 chopped garlic clove
1 chopped small strong pepper
sea salt and white pepper to taste

Cut the tofu into cubes.

Add the beans, corn and peppers. Set aside.

Mix the oil, tamari, juice of lime, garlic and strong pepper
in a bowl.

Add the vinaigrette to the tofu and mix well.

Adjust the seasonings to taste.

Serve with nachos and guacamole.

Mediterranean salad (Provence, France)

By ERIC BOUTIN

"All time favourite!"

Degree of difficulty*
Cost $
For 4 people
Preparation: 30 minutes
Note: Marinate for 4 hours

SALAD:
3 ounces or 90 g tofu cut into sticks
14 ounces or 400 g cooked pasta (short)
3 tbsp. or 50 g onion chopped finely
2 tbsp. or 60 g roasted red pepper, without skin and
        cut into strips
2 tbsp. or 60 g roasted yellow pepper, without skin and
        cut into strips
2 or 200 g zucchini cut into sticks
20 or 150 g fresh asparagus tips, blanched
1 tsp. or 100 g cucumber flesh cut into sticks
3 or 160 g dried, rehydrated tomatoes sliced into strips
12 or 40 g green string beans lightly blanched
12 to 18 tangerine sections
salt and pepper to taste

This recipe might be compared to a pasta salad, however,
here the pasta is in the minority and the vegetables dominate
to make a festival of flavour and beauty.

Preheat the oven to 450 degrees F (225 degrees C).

ROASTED PEPPERS:
Wash and place the peppers in the oven just until they are roasted.
Then place the peppers in a bowl. Cover with plastic wrap and let
them sweat. When they are cold, remove the skin and they are ready.

SALAD:
Mix all the ingredients and place in the refrigerator for 4 hours with
the vinaigrette. Stir from time to time.
Before serving, mix well and adjust seasonings to taste.
VARIATION:
Add feta cheese before serving.

VINAIGRETTE:
1/3 cup or 100 ml olive oil
1 tsp. or 5 ml sesame oil
4 tbsp. or 60 ml orange juice
2 tsp. or 10 ml freshly chopped oregano
3 tbsp. + 1 tsp. or 50 ml soya sauce (suggestion: Kikkoman)
1 tsp. or 5 ml strong mustard
1 tsp. or 5 ml cider vinegar (to taste)
3 tbsp. + 1 tsp. or 50 ml balsamic vinegar
Freshly chopped basil leaves

Mix all the ingredients well while beating vigorously. Set aside.

Warm spinach salad with mandarin tofu and warm goat's cheese (France)

By ÉRIC BOUTIN

Degree of difficulty*
Cost $
For 2 to 4 people

3¹/2 ounces or 100 g lardons (small pieces of bacon)
1/4 or 50 g finely sliced onions
1 tsp. or 5 g crushed garlic
70 g tofu cut into small cubes
5 tsp. or 25 ml balsamic vinegar
5 tsp. or 25 ml orange juice
2 ounces or 60 g drained bits of goat's cheese
9.6 ounces or 290 g washed spinach without stalks
12 Sections of fresh or canned tangerines (mandarins)

Heat the lardons in a pan just until coloured.

Add the onion, garlic and tofu. Mix well.

Add the vinegar and the orange juice. Remove from the burner.

Add the bits of goat's cheese and the spinach.
Mix vigorously to avoid

Cooking the spinach.

Place on plates and garnish with the sections of tangerines.

For a light, little dish at the beginning of a successful evening…

Rhapsody in green (Quebec)

By DENISE BOYTE

"My mother has, and has always had, the inborn sense of healthful food and a wonderful presentation."
-Frances Boyte

Degree of difficulty*
Cost $
For 2 people

VINAIGRETTE:
1/4 cup or 60 ml red wine vinegar
3 tbsp. or 45 ml olive oil
1 tbsp. or 15 ml lemon juice
1 crushed garlic clove
1 tsp. or 5 ml salt
1/2 tsp. or 2.5 ml dried marjoram
8 ounces or 250 g extra firm tofu
4 fresh asparagus
1 cup or 250 ml broccoli bunches
1 carrot cut into slices
1 cup or 250 ml chick peas
1/2 cup or 125 ml red onions cut into thin rounds
some leaves of spinach to decorate

Mix the vinegar, oil, lemon juice, salt and marjoram in a bowl using a whisk.

Add the tofu and delicately mix well to coat it.
Marinate for 20 minutes at room temperature.

Rinse and drain the tofu well. Next, place it in between 2 plates and place a weighted tin on top. Let sit for 20 minutes.

Next, cut the tofu in cubes of 1/2 inch or 1 cm.

Cook the asparagus, broccoli and carrots to the *al dente* stage. To cook them *al dente*, it is preferable to steam them separately and then quickly run them under cold water to stop their cooking.

Next, drain them.

In a salad bowl, add the marinated tofu, the cooked vegetables, the chick peas and the red onion. Mix delicately to coat all the ingredients. Cover and refrigerate for 30 minutes. Serve on a bed of spinach.

Warm salad with an exotic twist (Quebec)

By VÉRONIQUE JUNEAU

Degree of difficulty*
Cost $
For 4 people

2 garlic cloves
1 jalapeno pepper without seeds and sliced thinly
2 tbsp. or 30 ml fresh ginger
2 tbsp. or 30 ml tamari
1/4 cup or 65 ml water
2 tbsp. or 30 ml rice vinegar
2 tbsp. or 30 ml cilantro
1 tbsp. or 15 ml sesame butter*
2 tsp. or 10 ml sugar
1 pound or 500 g extra firm tofu, rinsed and well drained
4 cups or 1 litre chinese cabbage finely sliced
2 cups or 500 ml watercress leaves (without the stem)
1/2 cup or 125 ml alfalfa sprouts (if desired)

*Sesame butter and tehina are made from sesame seeds.
Sesame butter is made from unshelled seeds. It contains
more calcium than tehina which is made from shelled seeds.

Place the garlic, pepper, ginger and the tamari in a mixer.
Mix well just until all the ingredients are finely cut. Set aside.

Place one spoonful of the preceding mixture in a small bowl to
which you will add the water, rice vinegar, cilantro, sesame
butter, sesame oil and sugar.
Mix well and set this vinaigrette aside.

Cut the pound of tofu into 4 pieces. Place the pieces of tofu
between two plates.

Place a weight on top of the plate for about 30 minutes to press
the tofu.
Drain the tofu lightly.

Place the tofu in the ginger mixture (the first mixture that was set
aside) and coat all sides well.

In a non-stick pan, heat one teaspoon of sesame oil. Brown the
tofu just until golden on all sides. Set aside and keep warm.

Mix the cabbage and the watercress and divide onto four plates.
Place the tofu on the mixture of cabbage and watercress. Pour
the vinaigrette over the tofu. Garnish with alfalfa sprouts. Serve
immediately.

*Véronique Juneau has been a journalist in the field of arts for 7 years. Firstly,
she held the title of radio animator for the Energie network and now has the title
artistic critic for the Internet Showbiss.net (www.showbiss.net) site, the most
important entertainment site for the french speaking people of Quebec.*

The Main Dishes

Albondigas with tofu (Mexico)
(Traditonal Mexiccan Stew)
BY JOSÉ TROTTIER

"In the beginning, one placed uncooked rice in the meatballs and the rice cooked in the meat. This recipe is much easier to make."

Degree of difficulty*
Cost $
For 4 to 6 people

SAUCE:
1/4 cup or 65 ml safflower oil
1 cup or 250 ml thinly sliced red onions
1 cup or 250 ml thinly sliced red peppers
1 cup or 250 ml thinly sliced green peppers
4 chopped cloves of garlic
ground chili to taste
2 tsp. or 10 ml honey
a pinch thyme
8 cups or 2 litres crushed tomatoes

TOFU BALLS:
5 cups or 1.250 litres well drained tofu
1 cup or 250 ml cooked brown rice
1/4 cup or 65 ml tamari
1/4 cup or 65 ml yeast
1/4 cup or 65 ml natural peanut butter
1 cup or 250 ml chopped onions
1 tbsp. or 15 ml crushed chili
1 tsp. or 5 ml chopped garlic
1 tsp. or 5 ml thyme
1 egg

SAUCE:
Brown the onions in the oil.
Add the peppers, garlic and chili. Brown 2 minutes.
Add the honey, thyme and tomatoes.
Bring to a boil and simmer for 20 minutes.
Adjust seasoning to taste. The sauce must be very spicy.
Set aside.

Preheat the oven to 350 degrees F (175 degrees C).
Bring enough water to a boil to poach 4 cups or
1 litre of well drained tofu. Set aside.

Boil 1 cup or 250 ml of tofu for 1 minute
(to harden the tofu). Drain and press.

Mix the cooked tofu together with the uncooked tofu and
the rest of the ingredients to bind together into balls.
Form the balls into the size of an egg.
Place the balls on a cookie sheet and bake for 15 minutes.
Turn them over and cook again for 10 minutes.
Place the balls in the sauce and coat them well.

Serve with rice or black beans.

Stuffed eggplant (Turkey)
By BENOÎT PAQUET

"This dish opens the door to marvelous turkish gastronomy."

Degree of difficulty*
Cost $
For 4 people
Preparation: To be made the same day

4 small eggplants peeled and cut into two, lengthwise
olive oil for cooking
salt and freshly ground black pepper to taste
1/2 pound or 225 g tofu with fine herbs cut
          into cubes of 1 inch or 2.5 cm
1/2 finely chopped Spanish onion
4 finely chopped garlic cloves
5 red tomatoes hulled, seedless and crushed
2 tbsp. or 30 ml freshly chopped parsley
1 tsp. or 5 ml ground cumin
1 tsp. or 5 ml dried thyme

Preheat the oven to 400 degrees F (200 degrees C).
With the help of a spoon, remove one quarter of the pulp
of the eggplants.
Brush olive oil on the eggplants. Salt and pepper and place
them on a cookie sheet.
Cook in a hot oven for 8 to 10 minutes depending on the size.
When cooking is finished, set aside.
Salt and pepper the cubes of tofu and brown them on a brisk
heat in a small amount of olive oil. Set aside.
At a moderate heat, cook the onions until golden.
Add the garlic, tomatoes, parsley, cumin and thyme.
Cook at a moderate heat for 15 minutes uncovered.
Add the tofu cubes. Cook another 5 minutes.
Adjust the seasonings to taste.
Garnish the eggplants with the preceding preparation and cook
in the oven for 15 minutes.
Serve the eggplants accompanied by a semolina of couscous
cooked to your liking.

VARIATION:
Sprinkle with grated cheese and bake in the oven.

Vietnamese chicken balls with tofu (Vietnam)

By SÉBASTIEN LEBLOND

Degree of difficulty*
Cost $
For 4 people

1 pound or 450 g minced chicken
4 ounces or 120 g soft tofu
1 egg white
1 tbsp. or 15 ml fish sauce
1 tsp. or 5 ml marinated ginger
1 tbsp. or 15 ml coriander
1/4 tsp or 1.25 ml cinnamon
1/4 tsp. or 1.25 ml crushed pimento paste (harissa)
1 tsp. or 5 ml flour
3 green onions chopped finely
2 garlic cloves
salt and pepper to taste
peanut oil for cooking

Reduce all the ingredients to a purée, except the oil, in a blender (food processor).
Refrigerate this mixture for 1 hour.
Shape into balls coming from the mixture.
Heat oil and fry the balls one by one in a wok.
Serve with the peanut sauce of your preference or with teriyaki sauce.

PEANUT SAUCE:
1/2 cup or 125 ml peanut butter
1/4 cup or 60 ml soya sauce
1/4 cup or 60 ml lime juice
2 tsp. or 10 ml sesame oil
1 cup or 250 ml mayonnaise
1/2 cup or 125 ml freshly chopped coriander
1/4 cup or 60 ml chopped green onion

Mix all the ingredients and refrigerate.

Braised lamb and tofu oasis style (Algeria)

By BENOÎT PAQUET

"Varied textures and aromas blended together and a lively red wine from Algeria! What a delight! The desert will have an air of Eden!!"
-Didier Girol

Degree of difficulty*
Cost $$
For 4 people
Preparation: Can be made in advance

1 pound or 450 g well drained firm tofu cut
          into cubes of 3/4 inch or 2 cm
olive oil for cooking
1 pound or 450 g lamb shoulder cut into cubes
100 g whole almonds crushed coarsely
13 ounces or 400 ml veal or lamb stock
1 tbsp. or 15 ml concentrated tomato purée
1 tbsp. or 15 ml ground cumin
2 tbsp. or 30 ml honey
1 tbsp. or 15 ml crushed pimento paste (harissa)
salt and freshly ground pepper to taste
6 ounces or 200 g dried prunes, pitted and
          rehydrated in a small amount of warm water
3 tbsp. or 45 ml orange flower water

Preheat the oven to 350 degrees F (175 degrees C)

In a saucepan, cook the cubes of tofu seasoned with salt and pepper in a small amount of olive oil on a fast heat. Set aside. In the same saucepan, cook the lamb cubes seasoned with salt and pepper.

Add the almonds and fry quiokly for 2 minutes.

Add the veal broth, tomato purée, cumin, honey and crushed pimento paste (Harissa).

Cover and braise in the oven for around 40 minutes, just until the meat is tender.

Add the tofu and the prunes and braise again for 10 to 15 minutes. Adjust seasonings to taste.

When ready to serve, add the orange flower water.

Degree of difficulty***

Cost $$$

For 4 people

SAUCE:
sunflower oil for cooking
1 large chopped grey shallot
1 cup or 250 ml dry white wine
10 peppercorns
4 juniper berries
a pinch thyme
1 bay leaf
1 slice of orange (pulp and peel)
1 cup or 250 ml freshly squeezed orange juice
1 1/2 cups or 375 ml duck or veal brown stock
Grand Marnier and orange syrup to taste
3 tbsp. or 50 g sweet butter in cold cubes
              (optional, but very good)
salt and ground white pepper to taste
orange syrup to taste

BUTTER THICKENER:
2 tbsp. or 25 g of creamed butter mixed with
2 tbsp. or 25 g of flour

In a small, deep, heavy saucepan, heat a small amount of sunflower oil and cook the shallot for one minute on low heat.
Add the white wine, peppercorns, juniper berries, thyme, bay leaf and the orange slice. Simmer to reduce to almost dry (there must be 1 or 2 tbsp. or 15 to 30 ml of liquid).
Add the orange juice and reduce again to half.
Add the brown stock and bring to a boil. Remove from the burner and thicken the sauce with the butter thickener while whipping vigorously. Simmer for 15 minutes. Strain the sauce and flavour to taste with the orange syrup. Season with Salt and ground white pepper.
Mix the cold sweet butter bit by bit while whipping vigourously without heating it. Finish with a trace of Grand Marnier or any other orange based liquor. Set aside.

CANDIED ORANGE AND ORANGE SYRUP:
1 cup or 250 g honey
1 cup or 250 ml water
10 slices of orange of 1/4 of an inch or 5 mm in thickness

Place the honey, water and slices of orange in a small saucepan. Bring to a boil and cook gently for around 45 minutes. The cooking is finished when the orange peel is tender. Now you will have the orange syrup which you will need to tone down the acidity of the sauce (white wine and orange).

THINLY SLICED DUCK BREASTS:
1 pound or 500 g barbarie duck breast* with skin
10 ounces or 300 g firm well drained tofu, cut into slices of
              3 inches x 1 inch x 1 inch or 8 cm x 2 cm x 1 cm
salt and freshly ground white pepper to taste
sunflower oil for cooking
*Grain fed duck
Note: The Barbarie duck can be ordered in advance from your butcher or bought in speciality stores: Ferme Orléans, Saint Laurent,l'île d'Orléans.

Preheat the oven to 360 degrees F (180 degrees C)
With a small knife, cut a small square through the skin to the flesh and no more. In a deep thick pan, heat a small amount of oil, season the meat and place skin side down first. When the skin is well browned, turn the meat over and finish the cooking in the oven for 15 minutes so that the meat remains pink. When the cooking is finished, place the breast on a cutting board and let rest for 5 minutes before carving.
In the oven, cook the slices of seasoned tofu on a lightly oiled cookie sheet. Carve the duck breasts thinly and lengthwise. Coat the heated plates with the sauce and lay out the duck slices and tofu slices alternately in a fan shape. Add 2 slices of candied orange and serve.

Lamb kebobs and marinated tofu
(Middle East)

By ÉRIC BOUTIN

Degree of difficulty*
Cost $$
For 4 people
Preparation: 15 minutes
Note: Marinate for 7 hours

1 red onion
2 garlic cloves
1 branch of thyme
3 bay leaves
a pinch cayenne or chili pepper
2 cups or 500 ml extra virgin olive oil
2 lemons cut in slices
3 cloves
salt and pepper to taste

KEBOBS:
2 pounds or 1 kg boned leg of lamb, cut into cubes
3 various coloured peppers
4 red onions
1/2 cup or 350 g firm tofu cut into large cubes
2 tbsp. or 30 ml extra virgin olive oil

Prepare the marinade with 2 chopped onions, garlic, thyme, bay leaves, chili pepper, cloves and oil.

Marinate the slices of lemon and lamb cubes for 7 hours.

Cut the peppers and onions into cubes and mix them with the tofu in 2 tbsp. or 30 ml of olive oil.

Soak together for 2 hours separately from the meat.

Next, place the meat, tofu and vegetables alternately on skewers.

Cook the kebobs on a grill and moisten the meat from time to time with the marinade.

Iranian Kebobs and tofu (Iran)
By BENOÎT PAQUET

"You are going to realize that tofu can appear to be very exotic…And this will not be a mirage!"

Degree of difficulty*
Cost $
For 4 people
Preparation : Can be made the day before
Note : Appetizer or main dish

KEBOBS:
1 pound or 500 g well drained firm tofu cut into cubes
        of 1 inch or 2.5 cm
12 ounces or 350 g small green zucchini cut into slices
        of 1 inch or 2.5 cm
24 small cultivated mushrooms
1 Spanish onion cut into small squares of 1 inch or 2.5 cm
1 red pepper cut into cubes of 1 inch or 2.5 cm
8 whole cherry tomatoes
olive oil for cooking

Place 3 pieces of each ingredient on the skewers alternately and keep the cherry tomatoes for the centre of each kebob.
After the assembly of these 8 kebobs, oil them lightly and cook on a grill for 5 to 6 minutes on each side, just until they are well browned.

IRANIAN SAUCE:
12 garlic cloves split in half
1/3 cup or 100 ml fresh natural yogurt
2/3 cup or 200 ml creamy tofu
3/4 cup or 200 ml olive oil
2 tbsp. or 30 ml freshly chopped parsley
2 tbsp. or 30 ml freshly squeezed lime juice
salt and white ground pepper to taste

In a food processor chop the garlic coarsely.
Add the yogurt and tofu and blend about 30 seconds on high speed.
Always on high speed, pour the olive oil bit by bit; like making mayonnaise.
Mix in the parsley and lime juice and adjust the seasonings to taste.

Tofu, pineapple and kiwi kebobs
(Australia)

By JOSÉ TROTTIER

"The Asian influence shows up in Australia, where this marinade is used."

Degree of difficulty*
Cost $
For 4 to 6 people
Note: Prepare the marinade the day before

MARINADE:
juice of 2 limes
1/2 cup or 125 ml sesame oil
1 tsp. or 5 ml grated ginger
1 tsp. or 5 ml chopped garlic
1 tbsp. or 15 ml tamari
a pinch thyme
1 bay leaf

Mix all the ingredients to obtain a marinade.

BROCHETTES:
20 ounces or 600 g tofu cut into cubes
1 pineapple
4 kiwis

THE DAY BEFORE:
Marinate the tofu.

THE SAME DAY:
Trim the pineapple and cut into cubes.

Peel the kiwis, then cut into quarters.

Soak the wooden kebob sticks in cold water for 15 minutes to avoid their burning.

Place the food on the wooden kebob sticks alternating with tofu, pineapple and kiwi.

Cook the kebobs on the grill or in the oven for 15 to 20 minutes.

Serve the kebobs coated in the marinade sauce over a bed of brown rice.

Quail Marsala and tofu (Italy)
By BENOÎT PAQUET

Degree of difficulty*
Cost $$$
For 4 people
Preparation: Rather long

MARSALA SAUCE:
sunflower oil for cooking
1 large chopped grey shallot
3/4 cup or 200 ml marsala
10 whole grains black pepper
a pinch dried thyme
1 bay leaf
1 clove
1 1/2 cups or 375 ml veal brown stock
1/2 cup or 125 ml 35% cream, thick or double cream
salt and freshly ground white peppr to taste

QUAIL PREPARATION:
salt and freshly ground pepper to taste
8 quail breasts*
8 quail thighs*
4 slices of firm tofu with fine herbs
        of 2 inches x 3 inches or 5 cm x 7 cm
sunflower oil for cooking
*grain fed quail

In a saucepan, cook the shallot lightly in sunflower oil until golden.
Add the marsala, grains of pepper, thyme, bay leaf and the clove.
Boil down until there is 1 tbsp. or 15 ml of liquid.
Add the veal stock and simmer on low heat, uncovered,
for 20 to 30 minutes.
Add the cream and cook 2 to 3 minutes without letting mixture boil.
Strain the sauce through a sieve.
Salt and pepper. Keep warm and set aside.

Salt and pepper the breasts and thighs
Salt and pepper the tofu.
On a lightly oiled cookie sheet cook the tofu until well browned either in the oven or on the grill. Set aside.
Do the same with the breasts and thighs until the cooking is complete.
Prepare a vegetable accompaniment such as fresh green beans or some new potatoes in season.
Place on heated plates.
Coat the plates with the sauce and place the well browned tofu slices on the plates.
Add the quail breasts and thighs on the slices of tofu (artistically!).
Coat with the rest of the sauce.
Sit down and eat and play the mandolin!

Note: It is possible to soak the tofu slices in the marsala for a few minutes to give them a lovely colour and a very subtle aroma.

Tofu Koulibiac

(Koulibiac: A traditional Scandinavian and Russian dish.
Salmon is usually the main ingredient, however, in this recipe, it is replaced with tofu.)

By JOSÉ TROTTIER

"A glass of icy cold vodka, tzigane music and koulibiac...what could be better?"

Degree of difficulty*

Cost $

For 6 people

1/4 cup or 65 ml butter
1 chopped onion
1 package spinach
1/4 pound or 125 g mushrooms
1/4 cup or 65 ml white wine
a pinch nutmeg
2 sheets puff pastry
1 cup or 200 g cooked brown basmati rice
1 pound or 450 g silken, extra firm tofu
          cut into slices
2 hard boiled eggs cut into slices
sea salt and white pepper to taste
1 beaten egg

Preheat the oven to 400 degrees F (200 degrees C).

Brown the onions and spinach in one half of the butter.
Set aside.

Chop the mushrooms and brown them in the rest of the butter.

Add the wine, nutmeg and season.
Cook until all the liquid has evaporated. Set aside.

Place one sheet of pastry on a metal baking pan.

Cover the pastry with the rice while leaving a border of 1/2 inch or 1.25 cm without rice.

Add the slices of tofu, the spinach, the mushrooms and the egg slices.

Moisten the border of the pastry with a little water.

Cover with the second sheet of pastry.

Seal the borders and make two incisions in the centre of the pastry.

Brush with the beaten egg.

Bake for 30 to 40 minutes in the oven just until the crust is golden.

Serve with sour cream or with a Mellow Australian vinaigrette (recipe on page 104).

Chicken strips and tofu szechuan style (China)

By BENOÎT PAQUET

"Just as if you were at the great wall of China! It is happiness, and it is very healthy!"

- Didier Girol

Degree of difficulty*
Cost $$
For 4 people
Preparation: To be made the same day

SAUCE:
a pinch salt
a pinch freshly ground black pepper
2 tsp. or 10 ml corn starch (or potato flour)
3 tsp. or 15 ml soya sauce
3 tsp. or 15 ml rice vinegar or dry sherry
1 tsp. or 5 ml honey
1 cup or 250 ml chicken or vegetable broth

CHICKEN AND VEGETABLES:
safflower oil
1/2 pound or 225 g skinless chicken breasts without fat
  cut into strips
1/2 pound or 225 g well drained firm tofu cut into strips
  (like the chicken)
3 ounces or 100 g red pepper cut into strips
3 ounces or 100 g zucchini cut into strips
3 ounces or 100 g red onion sliced thinly
1 garlic clove finely chopped
1 tsp. or 5 ml freshly grated ginger

Mix all the dry ingredients in the sauce.
Gradually add the liquid ingredients and set aside.

CHICKEN AND VEGETABLES:
Brown the chicken strips and tofu, previously salted and peppered, in a small amount of safflower oil in a wok or deep heavy pan. Fry briskly while stirring constantly for 1 or 2 minutes, according to the thickness of the strips. Remove from the wok.

At a moderate heat, brown the pepper, zucchini, onion, garlic and ginger for 1 or 2 minutes in the baking juice.

Add the prepared sauce.

Bring to a boil while stirring constantly and add the chicken and tofu.

Serve hot with plain cooked rice.

Quiche with leeks, asparagus and tofu
(Canada)

By ÉLISABETH BÉLANGER

Degree of difficulty*
Cost $
For 4 to 6 people

PASTRY:
1/2 cup or 125 ml ice water
1/2 cup or 125 ml canola or sunflower oil
2 cups or 500 ml pastry corn flour
a pinch sea salt

QUICHE:
2 tbsp. or 30 ml olive oil
2 whites of leek
12 fresh asparagus or fiddleheads in season
2 eggs
2/3 cup or 170 ml natural soya beverage
1 package or 450 g well drained tofu
1/2 cup or 125 ml gruyère cheese
sea salt and fresh pepper to taste

In a mixer, stir the water and oil.
Add the flour and salt and mix well to form a ball. Add a small amount of water if needed.
Divide the ball in half (save one half in the freezer for later use).
Roll out the pastry (oil based pastry is more flexible than others).
Line a quiche mold of 10 inches or 25 cm in diameter.

Preheat the oven to 350 degrees F (175 degrees C).
In a small amount of olive oil on a medium heat, brown the leeks, that you will have previously washed, dried and cut thinly, for around 8 minutes. During this time, cook the asparagus or fiddleheads in boiling salted water.
Rinse under cold water and drain.
In a bowl, beat the eggs, soya beverage, well drained tofu and cheese. Season.
Garnish the bottom of the pie with the leeks and asparagus.
Add the egg mixture.
Cook in the oven for 30 to 40 minutes.
Savour with a green salad seasoned with a fresh herb vinaigrette.

Health, gastronomy and culture are the words locked into Élisabeth's vocabulary.

Fish pastry and tofu à la Sydney sauce (Australia)

By BENOÎT PAQUET

"Accompany this speciality with a little Australian white wine. And don't forget to have a toast to Sydney. It's in the bag!"
- (An old kangaroo joke) Didier Girol

Degree of difficulty*
Cost $
For 4 people
Preparation: Fairly long

8 sheets filo pastry
1/2 cup or 100 g melted butter for cooking and
     brushing on the filo pastry

FILLING:
1/2 spanish onion chopped finely
1 tbsp. or 15 ml butter
1/2 pound or 250 g cooked fillet of fish (your choice)
     without skin and bones
1/2 pound or 250 g medium firm tofu, well drained and
     cut into small cubes
1/3 cup or 100 g gherkin pickles marinated in aneth,
     cut into small cubes
1¹/2 cups or 200 g cooked rice
1 egg to glaze the filo pastry
1 tbsp. or 15 ml freshly chopped parsley
salt and freshly ground pepper to taste

SYDNEY SAUCE:
3/4 cup or 200 ml milk
1/3 cup or 100 g creamy tofu
1/3 cup or 100 ml 35% cream, thick or double cream
1/3 cup or 100 g grated cheddar cheese
grated nutmeg to taste
salt and ground white pepper to taste

BUTTER THICKENER:
2 tbsp. or 25 g creamed butter with 2 tbsp. or 25 g of flour

FILLING:
Preheat the oven to 400 degrees F (200 degrees C).

Brown the onion in a small amount of butter.
Mix together the fish, tofu, pickles, rice and parsley in a bowl.

Add the fried onion.
Salt and pepper.

Stack the sheets of filo pastry taking care to brush melted butter between each layer.

Spread the filling over the pastry and roll to obtain the shape of a cylinder.

Brush with the beaten egg.

Cook in the oven. Remove from the oven when the pastry is golden.

SYDNEY SAUCE:
In a deep, heavy pan, bring the milk, tofu and cream to a boil.

Remove from the burner and mix the butter thickener in vigorously with a whisk.

Simmer 15 minutes, stirring from time to time.

Add the cheddar, nutmeg, salt and pepper.

Serve the pastry directly onto the plates with the sauce, or on a serving platter with a gravy boat.

Tofu ravioli with yellow tomato purée

By LUC TROTTIER

"Buon appetitto!"

Degree of difficulty*

Cost $

For 12 people

Preparation: Fairly long

FILLING:

1/4 cup Olive oil
1/2 pound or 250 g green beans cut into
      pieces of 1/4 inch or 0.5 cm
1/2 pound or 250 g carrots cut
      into 3 mm cubes
1 broccoli processed in a blender
1 fennel bulb cut into cubes and
      the leaves chopped finely
1/2 pound or 250 g zucchini cut
      into small cubes
salt and pepper to taste
14 ounces or 400 g regular firm tofu processed
      in a blender
breadcrumbs

RAVIOLI PASTA:

2 cups or 500 g sifted or semolina flour
3 whole eggs
3 egg yolks
1 tbsp. olive oil
1/4 cup or 50 ml water

YELLOW TOMATO PURÉE:

50 ml olive oil
3 to 4 grey shallots
150 ml white wine
2 pounds or 1 kg skinned yellow
tomatoes cut into cubes
a touch of garlic
salt and pepper to taste
thyme and bay leaf to taste

FILLING:

Parboil the green beans just until they are tender but still crunchy.
Add the carrots, broccoli and fennel and stir frequently.
Do not cover, so that the vegetables retain their bright colours.
When the vegetables are well heated, add the zucchini cubes, which require less cooking. Season with salt and pepper while cooking.
Add the tofu and breadcrumbs last and place in the refrigerator to cool down for not less than 2 to 3 hours.

RAVIOLI PASTA:

Place the flour in a large bowl and make a hollow in the center.
Place the rest of the ingredients in the center and stir with a fork.
Gradually shape into a ball of dough and knead just until a smooth consistency is obtained. Add water or flour if needed.
Divide the dough into 2 balls. Roll out one ball to 1/4 of an inch or 0.5 cm in thickness.
Place 2 tsp. or 10 ml of filling every 2^1/$_2$ inches or 6 cm.
With the aid of a brush, lightly moisten with water between the spoonfuls of filling and on the borders.
Roll out the second ball and cover the layer of dough. With your hands, push down between each filling to remove any air bubbles. With a ravioli knife or a very sharp knife, cut into squares between each ravioli ball.

COOKING OF THE RAVIOLI:

Cook the ravioli in boiling salted water for 7 to 10 minutes.
Drain but do not rinse.

YELLOW TOMATO PURÉE:

Brown the grey shallots in a pan with olive oil and moisten with white wine.
Simmer the sauce to reduce it and add the yellow tomatoes and the rest of the ingredients.
Simmer at a low heat for around 30 minutes.
Place all the ingredients in a blender and then strain through a sieve.

THE SERVICE:

These ravioli can be served as appetizers or as a main dish.
Cover them with the yellow tomato purée. Garnish with diced tomatoes, green and red peppers. Decorate with a twig of aneth or fennel.

Luc Trottier has worked in cookery for 20 years, for the most part of which he has held the title of head chef. He is the founder of Pâtes arc-en-ciel inc., and he offers a selection of fresh pastas and fillings of a high quality and all colours and flavours. His pastas are made to order for chefs and restaurants.

Tofu mole poblano (Mexico)

By JOSÉ TROTTIER

"This uncommon recipe literally astounded me. When it is your turn, don't be afraid to blend the flavours and you too will be amazed."

Degree of difficulty**
Cost $$
For 8 people

2 red peppers
2 Hungarian peppers
1 cherry pepper
1 bird pepper (Tepin, Pequin)
2 cups or 500 ml chicken or vegetable broth
1/4 cup or 65 ml slivered white almonds
2 tbsp. or 30 ml sesame seeds unshelled*
1/4 tsp. or 1.5 ml coriander seeds
1/4 tsp. or 1.5 ml anise seeds
1 chopped onion
1 large tomato, peeled, seedless and cut into cubes
3 tbsp. or 45 ml raisins
1 chopped tortilla, 6 inches or 15 cm
1/2 tsp. or 2.5 ml chopped garlic
1/4 tsp. or 1.5 ml powdered cinnamon
1/4 tsp. or 1.5 ml powdered clove
1/2 tsp. or 2.5 ml sea salt
a pinch white pepper
3 tbsp. or 45 ml safflower oil
small piece of unsweetened chocolate
2 pounds or 1 kg sliced tofu

*unshelled sesame seeds have more calcium than
 shelled sesame seeds.

Scald the skins of the peppers and then remove the skins and seeds.

Soak the peppers in one half the broth for 30 minutes while boiling.

Reduce the almonds, one half of the sesame seeds, the coriander seeds, and the anise seeds to a powder using a coffee grinder. In a blender, add the peppers, broth, onions, tomatoes, raisins, tortilla, garlic, cinnamon, clove, the almond mixture and salt and pepper and reduce to a purée.

Heat 1 tbsp. of Safflower oil and add the purée.

Simmer for 5 minutes while stirring constantly.

Add the rest of the cold broth and the chocolate.
Cook on a gentle heat.

Heat the rest of the oil and fry the slices of tofu on each side.

Serve the slices of tofu coated with the sauce and sprinkle the rest of the sesame seeds over the dish.

Sagamité (American Indian, Canada)

(A traditional dish of the American Indians consisting mainly of corn flour.
In their time, one would eat it at breakfast with fruit and at supper with meat.)

By JOSÉ TROTTIER

"A bowl of sagamité, a chunk of bannock and a roasted poultry breast, and we will be taken back to the days of the pilgrims."

Degree of difficulty*
Cost $
For 4 people

4 cups or 1 litre chicken or vegetable broth
6 tbsp. or 80 ml corn flour
8 tbsp. or 90 ml cold broth
1 cup or 250 ml frozen corn kernels
1 package or 450 g tofu with fine herbs cut into cubes
1 tbsp. or 15 ml rice miso
white pepper to taste

Set aside 8 tbsp. of the broth and heat the rest.

Mix the flour with 6 tbsp. of the cold broth.

Add to the hot broth and bring to a boil while constantly stirring. Simmer for 10 minutes on a slow heat.

Add the tofu.

Add the miso, previously diluted in 2 tbsp. of the cold broth.

Cook without boiling for 1 to 2 minutes
Adjust the seasonings to taste.

Note: To vary this recipe, serve it with chicken, pork or lamb cubes that you would add to the broth, and accompany with vegetables like: turnip, rutabaga, carrot or parsnip.

Tofu méli-mélo with mild pepper creamed vegetables (International)

By BENOÎT PAQUET

"The delicate aroma of this vegetarian dish raises a symphony of champagne bubbles. What a marriage!"

Degree of difficulty*
Cost $$
For 4 people
Note: Vegetarian dish

SAUCE:

INGREDIENTS No 1
olive oil for cooking
1 large red pepper cut into cubes
2 tbsp. or 30 ml green of leek sliced thinly
1 tbsp. or 15 ml chopped grey shallot
1 tbsp. or 15 ml carrot sliced thinly
1 tbsp. or 15 ml celery sliced thinly
1 small piece garlic sliced thinly (less than a clove)

INGREDIENTS No 2
1/2 cup or 125 ml dry white vermouth
1 cup or 250 ml 35% cream, thick or double cream
2 tbsp. or 30 ml concentrated tomato purée
1 bay leaf
a pinch thyme
a pinch basil
a pinch ground cumin
salt and freshly ground white pepper to taste

Heat a small amount of oil in a covered saucepan and cook the ingredients in No 1 on a slow heat for 5 minutes. Stir frequently. Add the vermouth and reduce to one half.
Add the cream, tomato purée, bay leaf, thyme, basil and cumin. Bring to a boil and carefully cook, covered, for 5 to 6 minutes. Place in a mixer at high speed for 2 minutes.
Strain through a sieve. Add seasonings.

MÉLI-MÉLO:

20 small round carrots (or cut into rounds) cooked in boiling water with a bay leaf and salt.
20 zucchini pieces cut into rounds (or sticks),
        sautéed in olive oil.
20 small turnip rounds (or cubes), cooked in salted water
20 sugar peas cooked in salted water
20 thin green beans cooked in salted water
20 white or brown mushroom caps sautéed in olive oil
20 asparagus tips cooked in salted water
4 whites of small leeks braised in a small amount of olive oil
8 ounces or 225 g tofu with fine herbs cut into cubes, salted and
        peppered and sautéed in olive oil.

Coat 4 heated plates with the sauce.
Arrange the hot vegetables and tofu on the plates.
Serve hot, accompanied with a good champagne!

Green enchiladas with tofu (Mexico)

(Enchiladas: flat cakes made of coarse cornmeal)

By JOSÉ TROTTIER

"Imagine yourself by the poolside eating enchiladas...all that is missing are the mariachis!"

Degree of difficulty*
Cost $
For 4 people

GARNISH:
3/4 cup or 190 ml cream cheese
1 cup or 250 ml sour cream
1 chopped red onion
2 pounds or 1 kg well drained tofu

SAUCE:
6 small, strong green peppers (serrano type)
        (in place of green, use red)
1 pound or 500 g green tomatoes
        (in place of green, use red)
1 tsp. or 5 ml freshly chopped coriander
3 tbsp. or 45 ml vegetable broth
1 egg
sea salt and white pepper to taste

Preheat the oven to 350 degrees F (175 degrees C)
Mix the cheese and 3 tbsp. of sour cream in a blender.
Remove from the blender.
Add the onion and tofu to the previous mixture, mix well and set aside.

Boil down to a purée, the peppers, tomatoes, coriander and broth.
Add the rest of the sour cream, the egg and salt and white pepper to taste.Mix.

ENCHILADAS:
12 tortillas of 9 inches or 22.5 cm
2 tbsp. or 30 ml parmesan

Stuff the tortillas with the garnish.
Place the tortillas on a pastry sheet.
Pour the tomato sauce over the tortillas.
Sprinkle with parmesan. Bake for 30 minutes.

Tuna and escargot cannelloni and cooked gray sea-bream fish with virgin tomato sauce

By MARIE-CHANTAL LEPAGE

Degree of difficulty*

Cost $

For 4 people

Preparation in advance:
1 hour, 30 minutes

CANNELLONI:
4 sheets cannelloni pasta, 4 inches by 4 inches
1 pound or 500 g regular firm tofu
10 freshly chopped tarragon
3 dozen escargots
lemon peel (lemon zest)
3 eggs
salt and pepper to taste

Place the tofu in a blender for a few minutes and add the escargots near the end so they are coarsely chopped.

Place these ingredients in a bowl and with a spatula add the eggs one by one with the chopped tarragon, lemon peel (zest), and salt and pepper.

Spread out the sheets of pasta and garnish with the above mixture and roll to make four cannelloni.
Steam for five minutes and keep warm.

VIRGIN SAUCE WITH RIPE TOMATOES:
1/2 cup or 125 ml virgin olive oil
2 tbsp. or 30 ml sherry vinegar
2 ripe tomatoes, seeded and cut into small cubes
1 chopped garlic clove
salt and pepper to taste

Mix all ingredients and soak at room temperature for one hour.

GRAY SEA-BREAM FISH:
2 filets of scaled, gray sea-bream fish cut into four equal portions
olive oil
grey sea salt
freshly ground pepper

Place the cannelloni in the center of a dish.

Fry the sea-bream fish in very hot olive oil, salt and pepper and place them midway over the cannelloni.

Pour the virgin sauce over all and garnish with some fresh herbs.

Oriental Sauté (China)

By DR. MARIE-ANDRÉE PIGEON

Degree of difficulty*
Cost $$
Adjust according to the number of guests

"This healthful recipe can satisfy all tastes as you can add vegetables of your choice. You can also add chicken, shrimp or any other seafood. I will leave the quantities for you to choose according to your appetite and the number of guests you will have."

olive oil to taste
butter to taste
onions chopped finely to taste
red pepper chopped finely to taste
zucchini cut into cubes to taste
water chestnuts sliced to taste
fresh, finely chopped ginger (optional) to taste
cashews to taste
tofu cut into cubes to taste
spinach cut into strips to taste
bean sprouts to taste
cooked chicken cut into cubes or replace with shrimp
        or any other meat or seafood to taste
tamari sauce to taste

Note: you can also add other vegetables according to your taste.

Brown the onion and red pepper in olive oil.

Add all the other ingredients except the spinach and bean sprouts. Cook 10 minutes.

Add the spinach and the bean sprouts. Simmer 5 to 10 minutes.

Serve on a bed of rice.

Dr Marie-Andrée Pigeon has practised medicine for the past two years in Charlevoix. She recommends a global approach in matters of preventative health (healthy nutrition, exercise, spiritual dimension, etc.) Her patient-doctor relationship is based on research of the causes and origins of diseases (environmental, emotional, nutritional, etc.) Soon she will open a health clinic in Charlevoix, a centre which will group together health professionals such as nutritionists, psychologists, social workers, acupuncturists and osteopaths. She has chosen to establish herself in the exceptional environment of Charlevoix, in Saint-Fidèle, in order to practise the values that she recommends.

Teriyaki sauté (Japan)

By SÉBASTIEN LEBLOND

Degree of difficulty*
Cost $
For 4 people
Note: Marinate for 1 hour

MARINADE:
3 tbsp. or 45 ml soya sauce
1 tbsp. or 15 ml sherry or port
3 tbsp. or 45 ml white wine
4 tsp. or 20 ml liquid honey
4 tsp. or 20 ml concentrated beef broth
1/4 tsp. or 1.25 ml wasabi*
1 tsp. or 5 ml grated ginger
1 clove of garlic

1¹/₂ pounds or 700 g tofu thinly sliced into sticks
1 tbsp. or 15 ml corn oil
1 tsp. or 5 ml corn starch

*wasabi: very strong Japanese horseradish

Marinate the tofu for 1 hour in the refrigerator.

Strain the tofu and reserve the marinade.

Heat the corn oil in a wok or in a non stick frying pan.

Brown the tofu at a brisk heat for 5 minutes.

Add the marinade to the tofu and use corn starch to thin it down.

Simmer for 2 minutes.

Serve over rice and with sautéed vegetables of your choice.

Shabu-Shabu (China)

(Traditional Chinese Fondue)

By SÉBASTIEN LEBLOND

Degree of difficulty*
Cost $$
For 4 people

1/2 pound or 225 g rice vermicelli
2 pieces of kombu (seaweed)
1 pound or 450 g thinly sliced fillet of beef
1/2 pound or 225 g tiger prawns, peeled and deveined
1/2 pound or 225 g tofu cut into cubes
1/3 cup or 75 ml green onions in pieces of 3 cm
30 mushrooms
6 carrots cut into strips
6 cups or 1.5 litres water

Cook the vermicelli in salted boiling water.

Drain and set aside.

Rinse the seaweed.

Bring 6 cups of water to a boil.
Add the seaweed and boil for 30 seconds.

Strain while pouring the broth into a fondue pot.

Divide the remaining ingredients and place on plates.

Cook the food in the fondue pot.

Dip in your favourite sauce.

Tacos mexicali (Mexico)

BY BENOÎT PAQUET

"Enjoy this dish with a fresh light beer as the Mexicans do. The only thing missing will be the sombrero and the mariachis!"

Degree of difficulty*
Cost $$
For 12 to 14 tacos
Note : Prepare the tortillas in advance

20 ounces or 600 g well drained medium firm tofu
          cut coarsely
corn oil for cooking
13 ounces or 400 g lean ground beef
1 green pepper in strips
1 onion finely sliced
1 garlic clove finely chopped
2 red tomatoes hulled, without seeds and crushed
1 jalapeno pepper chopped finely
2/3 cup or 200 ml beef or vegetable broth
2 tbsp. or 30 ml concentrated tomato purée
1 tbsp. or 15 ml chili powder
1 tsp. or 5 ml oregano
6 ounces or 200 g grated cheddar cheese
salt and freshly ground pepper to taste
shredded lettuce
12 to 14 tortillas

Brown the seasoned tofu in a small amount of corn oil.
Set aside.

Fry the beef, green pepper, onion and garlic together until completely cooked.

Add the tomatoes and pepper and cook a few minutes at a moderate heat.

Add the broth, the tomato purée and the spices.
Salt and pepper.

Cook 5 minutes on a low heat. Stir occasionally with a wooden spoon.

Add the tofu and adjust the seasonings to taste.

Place the mixture on the tortillas, garnish with grated cheese and lettuce.

Fold the tortillas in two and they are ready!

Sesame tofu on soba noodles

By PHILIPPE BEAUREGARD

*"Right now, tofu cuisine is in fashion with Californians.
One can serve it after being cooked in the oven, on sandwiches, hamburgers, pasta or rice."*

Degree of difficulty*

Cost $

For 4 people

Note : Marinate for 30 minutes

MARINADE :
2 tsp. or 30 ml rice vinegar or saké
1¹/₂ tbsp. or 22 ml black bean sauce*
1 tbsp. or 15 ml tamari
1 tbsp. or 15 ml white sugar
1 tbsp. or 15 ml water

TOFU :
1 pound or 500 g well drained, rinsed, regular
       firm tofu cut into strips of 2¹/₂ inches
       x 4¹/₂ inches or 6 cm x 11 cm
1/4 cup or 60 ml rice wine or saké
2 tbsp. or 30 ml tamari
2 tsp. or 10 ml roasted sesame oil
8 ounces or 250 g soba noodles
2 cups or 500 ml watercress, washed
       and drained
1 cup or 250 ml green onions
2 tbsp. or 30 ml black bean sauce*
3 tbsp. or 45 ml unshelled sesame seeds

BLACK BEAN SAUCE:
Can be bought at stores specializing
in Asian products.

Mix all the marinade ingredients together. Marinate the tofu for 30 minutes in the refrigerator.

Cook the noodles *"al dente"* in boiling salted water.
Rinse and drain them and place in a salad bowl.
Remove the tofu from the marinade and drain.

Add the rest of the marinade to the noodles. Mix well. Also, add the watercress, green onions and the black bean sauce. Mix well and set aside.

Spread the sesame seeds on a board. Roll the tofu slices in the seeds to cover both sides.

In a non-stick pan, fry the tofu in the sesame oil on a medium heat until they are a nice golden colour.

Place the noodle mixture on 4 plates and add the sesame tofu. Serve immediately.

VARIATION :
You can also cook the tofu in the oven at 350 degrees F (175 degrees C) for 15 minutes and finish the cooking under the grill to obtain a nice golden colour.

WINE SUGGESTION :
Zinfandel or Australian Shiraz

Philippe Beauregard lived in Europe at the time of the "mad cow" disease problems. Since that time, the daily consumption of tofu in that region has increased quite substantially.

Creole style tofu from "City Club" (China)

By CHEF PATRICK BREAUX

"Savour creole cuisine with tofu!... Vive la Louisiane!"

Degree of difficulty*
Cost $
For 4 people

8 ounces or 250 g well drained, rinsed tofu with
     fine herbs cut into cubes
1/4 cup or 60 ml olive oil
1/2 cup or 125 g non salted butter
1 1/2 cups or 375 ml chopped onions
3/4 cup or 190 ml   peppers cut into cubes
1/2 cup or 125 ml chopped celery
1 1/2 cups or 375 ml freshly crushed tomatoes
1/4 cup or 65 ml crushed garlic
1 1/2 cups or 375 ml tomato sauce
1 cup or 250 ml water
1/2 tsp. or 2.5 ml tabasco sauce
salt and pepper to taste
1/2 cup or 125 ml chopped green onions
1/2 cup or 125 ml chopped parsley
6 cups or 1.5 litres cooked rice

In a deep heavy pan, brown the tofu in oil.
Remove the tofu and cut into cubes and set aside.
Remove the excess oil and add butter. Fry the onions, pepper and celery.
Add the tomatoes, garlic, tomato sauce, water and tabasco sauce.
Adjust the seasonings to taste and simmer for 40 minutes.
Add the tofu, green onions and parsley 10 minutes before the cooking is finished.
Serve over rice.

Patrick Breaux is a native of Lafayette, Louisiana. He began his career as a pastry chef at the Riverside Inn and then went onto The Landing Restaurant and Alexander's Gourmet Restaurant at the Lafayette Hilton. Since 1985, he has been in charge of the famous City Club of Lafayette, where he regularly integrates tofu in his dishes on the menu. Patrick Breaux has been the recipient of many awards, 30 of which have been culinary medals from the Acadiana Culinary Classic. He has also been chosen Chef of the year of the acadian chapter of the American Culinary Federation in 1994. In 1998, he received two gold medals and two bronze medals from the prestigious Best of Show Award.

Tofu à la king (England)

By JOSÉ TROTTIER

Degree of difficulty*
Cost $$
For 4 people

1/2 cup or 125 ml cashew or whole brown almond nuts
1 tbsp. or 15 ml sesame seeds
3 cups or 750 ml water
1/2 cup or 125 ml flour
1/4 cup or 65 ml safflower oil
1/2 cup or 125 ml chopped onion
2 cups or 500 ml tofu cut into cubes
1/2 cup or 125 ml red pepper cut into cubes
1/2 cup or 125 ml quartered mushrooms
1 carrot cut into cubes
1 cup or 250 ml frozen green peas
1/2 tsp. or 2.5 ml garlic powder
sea salt and white pepper to taste

Reduce the nuts and sesame seeds to a powder.

Mix the water, nuts, and sesame seeds and flour in a blender.

Place on the burner and let thicken.

During this time, brown the onions in oil.

Add the tofu, peppers, mushrooms and carrots to the onions.

Cook 2 minutes. Add the green peas and garlic powder.

Adjust seasonings to taste.

Add the hot sauce and serve over a bed of bulgur.

Chicken à la king: a European recipe developed by a french master chef while he was working at a court in England. Tofu à la king is a recipe developed by José Trottier.

Curry tofu (United States)

BY DRS. NICHOLAS PELLETIER AND TANE MCKEE

Degree of difficulty*
Cost $
For 8 people

1 pound or 500 g well drained extra firm tofu
       cut into cubes of 1 1/2 inches or 4 cm
1 tbsp. or 15 ml cornstarch
1 tbsp. or 15 ml corn oil
5 to 6 shallots sliced finely
3 tbsp. or 45 ml peeled ginger sliced finely
4 tsp. or 20 ml curry powder
1 tsp. or 5 ml cumin
1 tsp. or 5 ml lime peel
salt and freshly ground pepper to taste
1 1/2 pounds or 750 g small red potatoes cut in half
3 cups or 750 ml water
14 ounces or 420 ml coconut milk
1/2 pound or 225 g sugar peas
1 large red pepper cut into squares of
       1 inch or 2.5 cm
boiling water

Place the tofu and cornstarch in a large plastic bag.
Mix just until the cornstarch adheres to the tofu.

In a frypan, sauté the tofu cubes in a small amount of corn oil just until they turn golden. Set aside.

In a pot, cook one half the shallots and the ginger, cumin, lime peel, salt and pepper.
Sauté for one minute.

Add the potatoes, water and the coconut milk to the curry and bring to a boil stirring constantly.

Cover, reduce the heat, and simmer at a low heat just until the potatoes are tender, around 20 minutes.

Add the peas, red pepper and the tofu to the curry and bring to a boil over a gentle heat while stirring occasionally.

To serve, stir the curry and serve from the pot or keep on a low heat for your guests to serve themselves at their convenience.

The curry can be left on the stove for one hour, if necessary. Add boiling water if needed, to avoid sticking to the bottom.

If needed, check the temperature occasionally with a cooking thermometer and adjust the heat accordingly.

The temperature should be maintained above 140 degrees F (70 degrees C).

This main dish is quick to make and contains tofu high in protein and fresh vegetables. It is a substantial vegetarian dish that is a fantastic supper to have on busy evenings.

NUTRITIONAL INFORMATION :
portion based on 4 ounces or 120 g of tofu.

Protein	9 g
Fibre	5 g
Calories	270 kcal
Lipids	12 g
Sodium	222 mg
Carbohydrates	29 g
Cholesterol	0 mg

Dr. Nicholas Pelletier is a scientific researcher at Genetech Inc., in San Francisco (California), where he helps develop new medications to fight cancer and cardiac illnesses.

Dr. Tane McKee is a veterinarian caring for small animals. Both strongly recommend preventative health care practices and nutritional products.

Fried foie gras and caramelized mangos with maple syrup and tofu cubes

By MARIE-CHANTAL LEPAGE

Degree of difficulty *

Cost $$$

For 4 people

Preparation: 30 minutes

INGREDIENTS:
1 pound or 250 g foie gras
1 firm mango
12 white asparagus
1 leek, cut into fine strips
3 ounces or 100 g regular firm tofu cut
          into small cubes
3/4 cup or 175 ml maple syrup
salt and pepper to taste

—

Cut the piece of foie gras into four portions and keep in the refrigerator.

Pierce the mango at the thickest part and immediately remove the skin while sliding the knife as close to the skin as possible. Cut the mango into four equal portions and shape fanlike.

Sprinkle them with sugar and caramelize them under the grill.

Blanch the white asparagus in salt water for a few minutes, cool them and surround them with a border of previously blanched leeks.

Heat the maple syrup, just until syrupy, and add the cubes of tofu. Reserve.

Heat a pan and quickly fry the pieces of foie gras, which have already been salted and peppered on each side.

Reheat the mango along with the white asparagus and leeks.

Place the foie gras and the fan shaped mango in the center of a dish.

Pour the maple syrup sauce over all and garnish with the white asparagus and strips of leek.

Tofu with chanterelles, saffron sauce and small melons (Portugal)

By BENOÎT PAQUET

"A wonderful dish that will enliven a winter evening if you have taken care, as I, to have dried some chanterelles when they were in season."   - Didier Girol

Degree of difficulty: *
Cost $$$
For 4 people
Preparation: To be made the same day

SAUCE:
sunflower oil for cooking
1 large chopped grey shallot
3/4 cup or 200 ml port
5 peppercorns
a pinch dried thyme
1 bay leaf
1¹/₂ cup or 400 ml veal, brown stock
1/2 cup or 125 ml 35% cream, thick or double cream
a pinch saffron*
salt and freshly ground white pepper to taste

*choose a good saffron; that is a Spanish saffron.

BUTTER THICKENER:
2 tbsp. or 25 g of creamed butter mixed
        with 2 tbsp. or 25 g of flour.

FINISHING:
1/4 cup or 60 ml oil for cooking
        (suggestion: grapeseed oil)
14 ounces or 400 g well drained firm tofu, cut
        into cubes of 1 inch or 2.5 cm
9 ounces or 250 g fresh chanterelles
        (or dried and rehydrated according to the season)
salt and freshly ground white pepper to taste
12 balls* cantaloupe (or cavaillon)
12 balls* honeydew melon (or Spanish melon)
12 balls* watermelon

*withdraw the pulp with a melon baller

SAUCE:
In a small, thick bottomed pan, cook the shallot in a small amount of oil for about one minute.

Add the port, peppercorns, thyme and bay leaf and reduce to one half.

Add the brown stock and bring to a boil and thicken the sauce with the butter thickener while stirring vigourously.
Let simmer for five minutes.

Strain the sauce through a sieve.

Add the cream and the saffron to the sauce and bring to a boil again.

Salt and pepper to taste and set aside.

FINISHING:
In a frying pan, brown the tofu and chanterelles on a brisk heat.

Salt and pepper at the end of cooking, that is, when the 2 ingredients are a nice golden colour.

Pour the sauce on the plates.

Divide the tofu chanterelle mixture into 4 portions.

Arrange the melon balls artistically
(the melon balls must be at room temperature).

Spoon some sauce lightly over the tofu and chanterelles.

Add clusters of parsley and serve immediately.

Tofu in beer batter (Scotland)

By JOSÉ TROTTIER

"Beer batter is the main ingredient of Scottish fish and chips, hence the importance of Guinness® beer in this recipe."

Degree of difficulty*
Cost $$
For 4 people

BATTER:
5 eggs
1/3 cup or 85 ml safflower oil
3/4 cup whole wheat flour
1 tbsp. or 15 ml baking powder
a pinch salt
1/3 cup or 85 ml guiness beer

FRYING:
1 package or 450 g tofu with fine herbs
oil for frying

Crack 3 eggs into a mixing bowl.
Separate the other 2 eggs. Add the yolks to the bowl and set aside the whites.
Beat the whites at high speed just until they whiten.
Put the mixer at a low speed and add the oil, bit by bit.
Mix in the flour, baking powder and salt.
Add the flour mixture to the eggs in small quantities while alternating with the beer.
Make the mixture very smooth and remove from the bowl and set aside.
Place the egg whites in the bowl and beat until stiff peaks are formed.
Gently add the egg whites to the preceding mixture with a spatula.
Place in the refrigerator for 15 minutes.

Cut the tofu into strips of around 1/2 an inch by 1/2 an inch or 1.25 cm by 1.25 cm lengthwise.
Heat enough oil in a pan for frying.
Immerse the tofu strips in the batter and coat them well.
Cook the tofu strips in the oil until a nice golden colour.
Serve with fried potatoes.

Tofu sauté Korma Madras (India)

By BENOÎT PAQUET

"You can make this dish the same day if you don't have a choice, however, it is better reheated. This dish is very spicy as is often the way in Indian gastronomy, but with a little Tavel rosé, it will be nirvana!" - Didier Girol

Degree of difficulty*
Cost $$
For 4 people
Preparation: To be made the day before

1 pound or 500 g well drained firm tofu cut into sticks
    of 2 1/2 inches x 2 1/2 inches or 6 cm x 1 cm
sunflower oil for cooking
1/2 finely sliced onion
1 tbsp. or 15 ml fresh ginger
6 ounces or 200 g carrots cut into rounds
2 small green squash cut into sticks
6 ounces or 200 g thin green beans
4 garlic cloves chopped finely
3 tbsp. or 45 ml freshly chopped coriander
1 tbsp. or 15 ml curry
1 tsp. or 5 ml turmeric
1 tsp. or 5 ml red pepper
1 tsp. or 5 ml caraway
1 tsp. or 5 ml ground cumin
2 tbsp. or 30 ml concentrated tomato purée
3/4 cup or 200 ml coconut milk
3/4 cup or 200 ml natural yogurt
salt and freshly ground pepper to taste

In a large pan, cook the tofu in a small amount of seasoned oil until golden.

Set aside.

In the same pan, cook the ginger and onion until golden.

Add the rounds of carrots, squash sticks and the beans. Cover and cook on a low heat for 5 minutes.

Add the rest of the ingredients and cook another 5 minutes.

Add the sautéed tofu and cook for 1 minute.

Salt and pepper.

Serve hot.

Skewered scallops and tofu cakes with crushed tomatoes and pink peppercorn sauce

By MARIE-CHANTAL LEPAGE

Degree of difficulty *

Cost $$

For 4 people

Preparation: 30 minutes

INGREDIENTS:
12 large fresh scallops
some cooked spinach leaves (*al dente*)
3 ripe tomatoes
1/2 cup or 125 ml olive oil
1/2 onion, medium chopped
1 garlic clove, chopped
1 fresh thyme branch
salt and pepper to taste
1/2 tsp. or 2.5 ml sugar
3 ounces or 100 g firm tofu
1 chervil branch

SAUCE:
1/2 cup or 125 ml fish broth
1/2 cup or 125 ml white wine
2 chopped grey shallots
1 1/2 cups or 375 ml 35% cream
1 tsp or 5 ml pink peppercorns
juice of 1/2 lemon
salt and pepper to taste

Place three scallops per person on a skewer and set aside.

Poach the tomatoes for two minutes in hot water, then place them in cold water.

Skin the tomatoes and remove seeds. Cut the remaining tomato pulp into small chunks.

Lightly brown the chopped onions in a little olive oil and add the tomato chunks, garlic, thyme, salt and pepper, as well as the sugar. Let simmer for fifteen minutes.

During this time, cut the tofu into rounds (2 inches in diameter by 1/4 inch thick). Start with a slice of tofu, then a layer of spinach, followed by crushed tomato and top with another slice of tofu. Keep warm.

For the sauce, mix together the white wine, the broth and the shallots. Boil until almost dry and then add the cream. Remove from heat when mixture reaches the boiling point. Add the pink peppercorns and the lemon juice.
Season to taste.

Fry the skewered scallops quickly in very hot olive oil for one minute on each side.

Salt and pepper to taste.

Place the cake in the center of a plate and arrange the skewered scallops on top.

Coat with the sauce and decorate with a chervil branch.

Tortillas (Mexico)

By BENOÎT PAQUET

Degree of difficulty*
Cost $
For 12 to 14 tortillas
Preparation: Can be made in advance

Note: To be used for making tacos

2 1/3 cups or 600 ml masa barina (corn flour)
1 tsp. or 5 ml salt
1 1/2 cups or 375 ml cold water

Preheat the oven to 240 degrees F (120 degrees C).

Mix the flour and salt in a mixing bowl. Add 1 cup or 250 ml of cold water while stirring constantly.

Knead with your hands while gradually adding the rest of the water to obtain a firm dough that does not stick to your hands.
Divide the dough into 4 portions. With a rolling pin, roll the dough between 2 sheets of waxed paper to 3/8 of an inch or 1.5 cm in thickness.

Cut the rounds into 5 inches or 12 cm in diameter. Place each round between 2 sheets of waxed paper until ready to cook.

Cook the tortillas in a non stick pan for 2 minutes on each side, just until they are a nice golden colour.

Wrap 4 or 5 tortillas in aluminum foil and keep them warm in the oven.

It is possible to keep the tortillas warm in the oven for around 2 or 3 hours. To do this, wrap the tortillas in layers of ten in paper towel, then wrap in moist linen. Wrap all in aluminum foil. Before serving, lightly moisten each tortilla and place in the pan for a few seconds.

Chinese noodles (Quebec)

By JANICK FORTIN

Degree of difficulty*
Cost $
For 4 people

2 cups or 500 ml cooked noodles
          or 1 cup or 250 ml uncooked noodles
10 ounces or 300 g frozen broccoli or
          1 fresh broccoli (heads only)
1 tbsp. or 15 ml sunflower oil
1 tsp. or 5 ml fresh or ground ginger
1 garlic clove
1 tbsp. or 15 ml water
1/2 tsp. or 2.5 ml sugar
1/2 tsp. or 2.5 ml salt
1 onion cut finely
12 ounces or 360 g well drained tofu cut into cubes
thyme to taste
soya sauce to taste

Cook the noodles.

Steam the heads of broccoli or cook them in a small amount of boiling water for 3 to 4 minutes only.

Drain and run under cold water.

Heat oil in a pan. Add the ginger and garlic. Cook and stir for around 30 seconds.

Add the broccoli, water, sugar and salt. Stir well.

Remove from the burner and set aside.

Sauté the onions in a pan with oil.

Add the tofu seasoned with thyme and soya sauce.

Cook the tofu for 3 minutes.

Add the tofu and noodles to the broccoli.

Reheat for a few minutes.

Sandra's tofu lasagne

(Cajun country, Louisiana)

By SANDRA GONSOULIN

"Enjoy this dish with friends to the sound of cajun music!"

-Frances Boyte

Degree of difficulty*
Cost $
For 10 to 12 people
Preparation: Can be made in advance

1 pound or 500 g whole wheat or spinach lasagna
water for cooking the lasagna
2 pounds or 1 kg tofu, rinsed and well drained
2 eggs
1 tsp. or 5 ml sea salt
pepper to taste
1/2 cup or 125 ml fresh coriander
1/2 cup or 125 ml freshly chopped parsley
1 tsp. or 5 ml ground nutmeg
1 tsp. or 5 ml ground cinnamon
3 to 6 garlic cloves chopped finely
1 onion
1 large Spanish onion
4 cups or 1 litre fresh mushrooms, thinly sliced
2 to 3 tsp. or 10 to 15 ml olive oil
20 ounces or 600 g heads of fresh broccoli
2 to 3 cups or 500 ml to 750 ml tomato sauce
6 to 8 fresh tomatoes sliced finely
6 to 8 fresh zucchini sliced finely
2 red peppers
2 green peppers
2 cups or 500 ml parmesan

Preheat the oven to 350 degrees F (175 degrees C)
Cook the lasagna in boiling salted water. Rinse in cold water and drain.Set aside.

Put the well drained tofu in a mixing bowl. Add the eggs, salt, pepper, parsley, coriander, nutmeg and cinnamon.
Mix well and set aside.

In a large non stick pan, brown the onions and mushrooms in 2 tsp. or 10 ml of olive oil. Withdraw the excess liquid. Put this liquid in a bowl and let it cool for 10 minutes. Next, add the chilled liquid and mushrooms to the preceding mixture.
Cook the broccoli heads in a small amount of water, rinse under cold water, and drain them well. Add the broccoli heads to the preceding mixture.

Grease the bottom and sides of a pan (9 inches x 13 inches or 22.5 cm x 32.5 cm) for the oven. Begin by placing the tomato sauce in the pan, then top with the lasagna, half the tofu mixture, the tomatoes, the zucchini, the Spanish onion and the peppers. Sprinkle with parmesan.
Repeat the procedure and finish with lasagna noodles on top. Then, sprinkle parmesan cheese and the rest of the tomato sauce.

Cook in the oven for 45 minutes. Let cool for 15 minutes before cutting.

Blue finn tuna carpaccio with sunflower oil and tamarillo

By MARIE-CHANTAL LEPAGE

Degree of difficulty**

Cost $$

For 4 people

Preparation in advance:
2 hours, 30 minutes

INGREDIENTS:
16 ounces or 500 g blue finn tuna
10 ounces or 300 g regular firm tofu
1 cup or 250 ml sunflower oil
2 tbsp. or 30 ml Tamari sauce
2 chopped grey shallots
1 tamarillo peeled, seeded and finely chopped
1 ounce or 30 g tomato skin cut in small pieces
1 ounce or 30 g yellow pepper cut into
          small pieces
juice of 1 lime
grey sea salt
freshly ground pepper
fennel branches

Mix the shallots, the tomatoes and the yellow pepper with the purée of tamarillo, the lime juice and the tamari sauce.

Add the sunflower oil, salt and pepper.

Refrigerate for two hours.

Thinly slice the tofu, as well as the blue finn tuna.

Spread a thin layer of tofu on each plate and cover with the tuna on top.

Coat generously with tamarillo oil and garnish with fennel branches.

Italian pasta (Quebec)

By DR. MICHEL ROBITAILLE

Degree of difficulty*
Cost $
For 4 people
Preparation: 1 hour
Note: 6 hours to cook

1/4 cup or 60 ml olive oil
3 cups or 750 ml thinly sliced onions
16 ounces or 450 g tofu with fine herbs
1/4 cup or 60 ml worcestershire sauce
2 cups or 500 ml thinly sliced celery
4 garlic cloves chopped finely
2 pints or 1 litre sliced mushrooms
4 cups or 1 litre grated vegetables
        (carrot, broccoli, zucchini, spaghetti squash)
84 ounces or 2.2 litres canned Italian tomatoes
48 ounces or 1.2 litres vegetable juice
5 1/2 ounces or 160 ml tomato paste
jalapenos to taste
1 cup or 250 ml split green peas (optional)

Preheat the oven to 250 degrees F (130 degrees C).

Brown the onion in the olive oil. Add grated tofu and Worcestershire sauce.

Add all the ingredients and cook in the oven in a cast iron container (preferably) for 6 hours.

This sauce freezes well and will be ready for spaghetti, linguine, macaroni, and lasagne.

Rice flour pasta (without gluten) with tofu and dried tomatoes (Quebec)

By DENIS PELLETIER

"This recipe is ideal for people who suffer from Celiac disease (intolerance to gluten). Naturally you can use any other kind of pasta. Try this recipe with home-made pasta that you have made yourself!"

Degree of difficulty*
Cost $

olive oil to taste
butter to taste
garlic from the garden to taste
home-made pesto to taste*
tofu cut into small cubes or julienne style to taste
black olives cut into slices to taste
capers to taste
home-made dried tomatoes to taste**
fresh basil from the garden to taste
Italian tomatoes or fresh from the garden to taste
home-made pasta or rice flour pasta to taste
parmesan reggiano cheese freshly grated to taste

*home-made pesto: olive oil, garlic, basil, parmesan, parsley and pine nuts blended in a blender.

**home-made dried tomatoes: tomatoes from your garden that you have dried yourself and let soak for many days in a preserving jar with olive oil, a little garlic and some basil.

In a large, slightly deep pan (cast iron) fry one or two garlic cloves in butter and olive oil at a medium heat.
Add the pesto, tofu, black olives, capers and the dried tomatoes. Let soften for a few minutes.
Add the basil and the fresh tomatoes that you have already crushed in your hands. If you do not have fresh tomatoes, use a large can of tomatoes and crush over the pan. Keep an eye on the sauce to adjust the consistency in proportion as it boils down. Boil the sauce down at a low heat for around 15 to 20 minutes while stirring occasionally.
Cook the fresh pasta in a large pot of water with a small amount of salt and 2 tablespoons of oil.
Drain the pasta and add the sauce.
Mix well and cook for a few minutes in order to reheat the pasta and absorb the taste of the sauce.

Retired from the Canadian Space Agency, Denis Pelletier assists his wife in a medical office. He is founding president of the Economic Development Committee of Saint Siméon. He is honorary aide de camp for the Honourable Lise Thibault, Lieutenant-governor of Quebec. Also, he practices the detection of harmful waves (geobiology) in order to allow people a better sleep at night and a better quality of life. Furthermore, he gives conferences on this topic so as to demystify it, and he conveys the detection of these harmful waves to everyone.

The Sauces & Accompaniments

Peanut sauce *(Vietnam)*

By SÉBASTIEN LEBLOND

Degree of difficulty*
Cost $
For 4 people

SAUCE:
1/2 cup or 125 ml peanut butter
1/4 cup or 60 ml soya sauce
1/4 cup or 60 ml lime juice
2 tsp. or 10 ml sesame oil
1 cup or 250 ml mayonnaise
1/2 cup or 125 ml freshly chopped coriander
1/4 cup or 60 ml chopped green onion

Mix all the ingredients and refrigerate.

This sauce goes well with Vietnamese chicken balls with tofu (recipe on page 67)

Tomato sauce *(Quebec)*

By SÉBASTIEN LEBLOND

Degree of difficulty*
Cost $
For 4 to 6 people

3 cups or 750 ml fresh skinned Italian tomatoes
2 garlic cloves
3 tbsp. or 45 ml freshly cut basil
2 tbsp. or 30 ml olive oil

Place the tomatoes in a blender and reduce to a puree.

Add the garlic, basil and olive oil.

Heat and serve with the *stuffed peppers* (recipe on page 37).

Tzatziki sauce *(Quebec)*

By SÉBASTIEN LEBLOND

Degree of difficulty*
Cost $
For 1 cup or 250 ml of sauce

3/4 cup or 175 ml sour cream
1/4 cup or 60 ml natural yogurt
3 garlic cloves peeled and chopped
1 tbsp. or 15 ml lemon juice
1 tsp. or 5 ml olive oil
1 tsp. or 5 ml raspberry vinegar
2 tbsp. or 30 ml chopped parsley
1 tbsp. or 15 ml fresh gherkins cut into cubes

Mix all the ingredients in a bowl and refrigerate one hour before serving.

It goes well with the *lamb kabobs and marinated tofu* (recipe on page 70).

Arlequin sauce with tofu and raspberries (Quebec)

By ÉRIC BOUTIN

Degree of difficulty*
Cost $
For 2 cups or 500 ml of sauce

2 tbsp. or 60 ml sunflower oil
1/3 cup or 70 g onion
1 tsp. or 5 g chopped garlic
2 tbsp. or 30 g raisins
2 tbsp. or 30 ml balsamic vinegar
1/4 cup or 60 ml soya sauce (suggestion: Kikkoman)
1 tbsp. or 15 ml tomato paste
1 1/3 cups or 325 ml demi-glace (fresh or packaged)
1/2 cup or 125 ml water
8 drops green tabasco
2 tbsp. or 30 ml concentrated juice from
         deep frozen raspberries (or berries from the field)
1/4 cup or 55 g tofu cut into cubes

In a small pan, fry the onions, garlic and the raisins in oil just until you have a light colour.

Add the vinegar and the soya sauce and cook lightly for a few seconds.

Add the tomato paste, demi-glace, water, Tabasco and the raspberry juice and bring to a boil.

Place the ingredients in a mixer and then strain through a sieve.

Add the tofu cubes. Set aside to cool just until ready to serve.

This sauce goes well with tofu steaks or tofu cooked in the oven.

It can also be used as a marinade for your favourite meat. It keeps well in the refrigerator for around 10 days in an airtight container.

Anchovy sauce (Greece)

By ÉRIC BOUTIN

Degree of difficulty*
Cost $$
For 4 people
Preparation: 30 minutes

3/4 cup or 200 ml extra virgin olive oil
1/2 cup or 100 g onion chopped finely
2 tbsp. or 30 g chopped garlic
2 tbsp. or 30 g pine nuts
2 fillets anchovies
Anchovy oil (quantity from the tin of anchovies)
4 tbsp. or 60 g tofu chopped finely
4 tbsp. or 60 g chopped capers
1/2 cup or 125 g pitted, chopped black olives
11 ounces or 330 g whole tomatoes in the tin
         well drained and crushed
1/2 cup or 100 g dried, rehydrated tomatoes
         sliced into strips

Fry the onion, garlic, pine nuts, anchovies and tofu in oil until golden.

Place in a bowl and add all the other ingredients.

Refrigerate just until ready to serve.
It is preferable to serve this sauce hot.

This sauce goes very well with fish and pasta.

Fast, simple…but how efficient!

Tofu pesto (France)

By SÉBASTIEN LEBLOND

"The mellow flavour of this vinaigrette will make you forget about commercially prepared vinaigrettes"

Degree of difficulty*
Cost $$
For 2 cups or 500 ml of mixture

6 ounces or 180 g fresh basil
1 ounce or 30 g pine nuts
3 ounces or 90 g grated parmesan
1/2 cup or 125 ml olive oil
1 tsp. or 5 ml lemon juice
6 Garlic cloves
1 ounce or 30 g firm tofu cut into small cubes of 2 mm
black pepper to taste

Place all the ingredients, except the tofu, in a blender.

Mix just until a smooth paste is obtained.

Add the tofu and mix with a spatula.

Serve with your favourite pasta, or as an accompaniment for grilled vegetables or fresh tomatoes.

Andalusian tofu (Spain)

By BENOÎT PAQUET

*"You can serve this delicious dish with a rice pilaf or simply with a good wild rice.
Spain is at your door and the evening will be filled with warmth!"*

-Didier Girol

Degree of difficulty*
Cost $$
For 4 people
Preparation: To be made the same day
Note: Appetizer or vegetable accompaniment

1 pound or 500 g firm, well drained tofu cut into cubes
            around 1 inch or 2.5 cm
2 cloves of garlic finely chopped
1/2 cup or 125 ml dry white wine
a pinch Spanish saffron
2 bay leaves
a pinch dried thyme
olive oil for cooking
1 green pepper cut into strips
1 red pepper cut into strips
1/2 Spanish onion finely sliced
2 tomatoes, hulled, seedless and crushed
salt and freshly ground pepper to taste

On a glass, or stainless steel (to avoid oxidation) serving platter, place the tofu, garlic, white wine, saffron and the bay leaf. Salt lightly.

Let soak for 20 to 30 minutes while stirring 2 or 3 times.

In a deep, thick pan, (or a non stick pan), brown the pepper strips and onion in a small amount of olive oil.

Add the crushed tomatoes and simmer for 2 minutes.

Next, add the ingredients that have been soaking and simmer for 10 minutes uncovered.

Adjust seasonings to taste.

Small stuffed vegetables (Quebec)

By FRANCIS CHAMPION

Degree of difficulty*
Cost $
For 4 people

5 onions
100 ml olive oil
4 medium-sized tomatoes
1 cup or 200 g wheat semolina
1/3 cup or 100 ml vegetable or chicken broth
3 ounces or 100 g miranda cheese
1 cup or 100 g black olives
thyme, oregano, basil, fine salt, ground white pepper,
        basil leaves, light soya sauce to taste
4 zucchinis
4 mushroom caps
4 artichoke hearts
1 1/4 cups or 100 g breadcrumbs

Preheat the oven to 350 degrees F (175 degrees C).
Blanch 4 onions for 3 minutes and cut the fifth onion finely and fry in olive oil until golden.
Add the crushed tomatoes then the semolina previously expanded in the broth.
Add the grated cheese and the thinly sliced , pitted olives.
Adjust the seasonings to taste.
Place the onions, zucchini, mushroom caps, and the hollowed out artichoke hearts on a cheese topped dish for the oven.
Stuff them with the mixture, sprinkle with olive oil and then breadcrumbs.
Cook in the oven for 25 minutes.
Serve an assortment of vegetables on each heated plate and garnish with a branch of basil.

With a diploma from the school of hotelier in Paris, Francis Champion has travelled across the world on passenger liners for the Hilton International chain. Chief cook, teacher of the fundamentals of cooking, a promoter of hygiene and healthiness, he has taught cooking at the Jacques-Rousseau Professional Development Center in Longueuil for the past ten years.

Tofumayo (United States)

By JOSÉ TROTTIER

"I have been conquered by silken tofu. I use it here in this mayonnaise-like sauce which keeps very well."

Degree of difficulty*
Cost $
For 2 cups or 500 ml of sauce

1 package or 350 g extra firm silken tofu
1/3 cup or 80 ml water
2 tbsp. or 30 ml lemon juice
1/2 tsp. onion powder
1/4 tsp. garlic powder
1/3 tsp. sea salt
1 tsp. or 5 ml strong mustard
3 drops tabasco
sea salt and white pepper to taste

Mix all the ingredients in a blender.

Adjust seasonings to taste.

Refrigerate.

Tofumayo: a vegetarian cuisine creation of the 70's.
It is a tasty replacement for mayonnaise.
Tofumayo can be used as a vinaigrette or as a dip.
You can vary the flavours by adding herbs (for example, chives, shallots, aneth) and spices such as curry, cumin and Cayenne pepper.

Mellow Australian Vinaigrette (Australia)

By JOSÉ TROTTIER

Degree of difficulty*
Cost $
For 1 cup or 250 ml of sauce
Preparation: Can be made in advance

6 ounces or 180 g soft silken tofu
1/2 peeled and pitted avocado
1 tbsp. or 15 ml lemon juice
1/4 cup or 60 ml water
1/2 tsp. or 2.5 ml sea salt
1/4 tsp. onion powder
1/4 tsp. garlic powder
1 tsp. or 5 ml fresh basil
1 tsp. or 5 ml chopped celery leaves
a pinch pepper

Mix the tofu, avocado, lemon juice, water, sea salt, onion powder and garlic powder in a blender.

Take the mixture out of the blender.

Add the basil and celery leaves. Mix with a spoon.

Adjust the seasonings as needed.

Let sit at room temperature before using.

Emulsion based vinaigrette (Quebec)

By BENOÎT PAQUET

Degree of difficulty*
Cost $
For 4 cups or 1 litre of sauce
Preparation: Can be made in advance

2 egg yolks
1 tbsp. or 15 ml strong mustard
a pinch dried thyme
a pinch dried basil
1 cup or 250 ml wine vinegar
        (white or red according to the colour of choice)
a dash garlic chopped finely
2 shallots chopped finely
salt and freshly ground pepper to taste
1 cup or 250 ml olive oil
1 cup or 250 ml sunflower oil
8 ounces or 250 g creamy tofu
2 to 3 tbsp. or 30 to 45 ml maple syrup

Note: Make this recipe with a beater or in the blender from start to finish. Prepare yourself if you are making it by hand!

Beat the yolks and the mustard or place them in a mixer.

Add the thyme, basil and a small amount of vinegar.

Add the garlic, shallots, salt and pepper.
Mix well to dissolve the salt.

Add the remaining vinegar gently in trickles.

Mix the vinaigrette with the olive oil and sunflower oil.

Add the creamy tofu and mix well to obtain a smooth vinaigrette.

Add the maple syrup to reduce the acidity of the vinaigrette and give them a little taste of Quebec.

VARIATIONS:
You can add tomato paste, Indian flavoured with 2 pinches of curry, or you can add fine herbs of your choice to your taste.

For an Italian sauce, add a small amount of parmesan.

This vinaigrette keeps well for 1 week in the refrigerator.

Bannock with tofu (American Indian, Canada)

By JOSÉ TROTTIER

"What could be more comforting than hot bannock on a winter evening or out camping."

Degree of difficulty*
Cost $
For 4 people

4 cups or 1 litre Durum wheat flour
1 1/2 tsp. or 7.5 ml sea salt
2 tbsp. or 30 ml commercial baking powder
1 1/4 cups or 310 ml tofu with fine herbs cut into cubes
1/4 cup or 65 ml peanut oil
2 cups or 500 ml water
corn or wheat semolina as needed

Preheat the oven to 400 degrees F (200 degrees C).

Mix the flour, salt and the baking powder.

Add the well drained tofu.

Add the oil and water. Sprinkle with a little flour if the dough is sticky.

Sprinkle some semolina on the bottom of a metal baking sheet.

Shape the tofu mixture into an oval ball and place on the baking sheet. Bake in the oven for 50 to 60 minutes.
Serve with salmon or smoked sturgeon.

Bannock: American Indian bread. Originally, one cooked this bread on a flat, hot stone or wrapped it around a stick to be held over a wood fire.

Scones with cheddar and tofu (Great Britain)

By JOSÉ TROTTIER

"Scones and tea, that is bliss!"

Degree of difficulty**
Cost $
For 12 scones

1 cup or 250 ml light wheat flour
1/4 tsp. sea salt
1 tsp. or 5 ml dried mustard
4 tsp. or 20 ml baking powder
1/4 cup or 65 ml softened butter
1/2 cup or 125 ml yellow grated cheddar cheese
1/4 cup or 60 ml crumbled tofu
2/3 cup or 165 ml milk

Preheat the oven to 450 degrees F (225 degrees C).

Mix the flour, salt, mustard and baking powder.

Cut the butter into the flour by using two knives just until the mixture becomes homogeneous.

Add the cheddar and tofu. Mix.

Make a well in the centre and add the milk.
Knead the dough for 2 minutes.

Shape into a ball and roll out until 1/2 an inch or 1.25 cm in thickness.

Cut into circles of 2 inches or 5 cm in diameter.

Place on a greased pastry sheet. Leave 1 inch or 2.5 cm of space between each scone. Cook for 15 minutes.

The Desserts

Crème brûlée with Morello cherries and tofu

By SÉBASTIEN LEBLOND

Degree of difficulty***

Cost $$$

For 12 people

24 Morello cherries in alcohol*
10 egg yolks
1/3 cup or 100 g creamy tofu
2³/4 cups or 700 ml 35% cream
2/3 cup or 200 g granulated sugar or fructose
1 vanilla pod cut in half
natural brown sugar to taste

*Morello cherries: can be replaced with
 summer berries or less expensive small fruit.

Preheat the oven to 350 degrees F (175 degrees C).

Place two cherries in each ramekin.

Beat the egg yolks with 1/3 cup or 100 g of sugar until white.

Add the well beaten tofu.

Mix the rest of the sugar, the vanilla pod and the cream in a pot and bring to a boil. Withdraw the vanilla pod and scrape the insides into the mixture.

Add the cream mixture to the egg yolk, sugar and tofu mixture.

Pour into ramekins.

Place the ramekins in a dish with hot water in it and cook for 30 to 40 minutes.

Cool well.

Sprinkle with brown sugar and place under the grill to caramelize.

An ultra rich dish for exceptional evenings!

Tofu tiramisu (Italy)

By SÉBASTIEN LEBLOND

Degree of difficulty*
Cost $$$
For 10 people
Preparation: To be made the day before

2 eggs
3 1/2 ounces or 100 g creamy tofu
1 cup or 300 g mascarpone
3 1/2 ounces or 100 g granulated sugar or fructose
vanilla to taste
2 cups or 500 ml 35% cream, thick or double cream
1 cup or 250 ml espresso coffee or very strong coffee
5 tsp. or 25 ml bailey's coffee cream
20 lady finger biscuits
cocoa powder to taste

Beat the eggs, tofu, mascarpone, sugar and vanilla until a creamy consistency is obtained. Set aside.

Beat the cream.

Mix the beaten cream with the preceding mixture. Set aside.

Fill the bottom of a mold container with one half of the mixture.

Mix the coffee and the Bailey's coffee cream together. Soak the lady fingers in this mixture. Place on the mascarpone mixture.

Cover all with the remaining mascarpone mixture

Sprinkle with cocoa.

Refrigerate for 4 hours. Serve.

For a special presentation, serve in martini glasses rather than from the mold.

Poached tofu in wine (France)

By JOSÉ TROTTIER

"I love this recipe that has the taste of spiced wine. A dessert to have as a special treat one evening of the week!"
-Frances Boyte

Degree of difficulty***
Cost $
For 4 people

3 cups or 750 ml red wine
1 cinnamon stick
1/2 orange in slices
3 juniper berries
2 black pepper seeds
1 clove garlic
450 g firm tofu

Place the wine, cinnamon, orange slices, juniper berries, pepper seeds and clove in a pot.

Bring to a boil, lower the heat and simmer for 5 to 10 minutes.

Cut the tofu into 4 cubes.

Poach the tofu in the wine mixture at a low heat for 15 minutes.

Leave the tofu to cool down in the wine.

Serve with whipped cream or a fruit sorbet.

Black cherry mousse (Germany)

By JOSÉ TROTTIER

Degree of difficulty**
Cost $$
For 4 people

1 tbsp. or 15 ml powdered gelatin
1 cup or 250 ml black pitted cherries
1/2 cup or 125 ml milk
2 egg yolks
3 tbsp. or 45 ml honey
1/2 cup or 125 ml sour cream
2/3 cup or 170 ml silken extra firm tofu

Soak the gelatin in a small amount of the cherry juice.

Bring the milk to a boil.

Beat the egg yolks with the honey until frothy.

Add the hot milk bit by bit.

Cook on a slow heat while stirring for 4 to 5 minutes. Remove from the burner.

Add the gelatin and stir to dilute it.

Leave to cool down without letting it set.

Beat the tofu to make it into cream.

Add the sour cream and tofu to the cherry mixture. Mix gently.

Cover with plastic wrap and let it blend together there. Allow it to set for at least 3 hours.

Fresh fruit salad (Quebec)

By ANNE DAVID

"With a novel twist... and some magic..."

Degree of difficulty*
Cost $$
For 4 to 6 people

Your favorite fruit salad recipe or

My suggestion:
3 oranges
1 grapefruit
1 apple
1 mango
1 kiwi
Fresh strawberries or raspberries to taste

1/2 cup or 125 ml maple liqueur (Sortilège)
1/2 cup or 125 ml firm tofu cut into
        cubes of 1/2 inch or 1 cm

To your favorite fruit salad recipe, add 1/2 cup or 125 ml of maple liqueur and 1/2 cup or 125 ml of firm tofu cut into cubes for 3 cups or 750 ml of fruit salad.

A creation of the moment in collaboration with Dominique Tremblay, a chef at Café Massawippi.

Strawberry mousse

By OLIVIER BEAUREGARD

"You do not have to be afraid of tofu. There is a way of making it discreet!"

Degree of difficulty*

Cost $

For 4 to 6 people

1/2 pound or 227 g silken tofu
3 tbsp. or 45 ml honey
1 pound or 454 g strawberries
juice of 1/2 lemon
1 cup or 250 ml 35% cream,
        thick or double cream
6 fresh strawberries

Place the tofu, honey, strawberries and lemon juice into a blender and reduce to a uniform, creamy purée.

Set aside.

In a medium sized bowl, beat the cream until firm.

Add the fruit mixture to the whipped cream.

Fill 4 to 6 dessert dishes with this mousse and decorate with fresh strawberries.

Keep in the refrigerator for 1 hour before serving.

Chocolate pie with tofu (Quebec)

By YVON TREMBLAY AND FRANCES BOYTE

"An amazing recipe, one of the treasures of "La Magie du tofu!"

Degree of difficulty*
Cost $
For 4 to 6 people

1 pie crust (graham crumbs)

GARNISH:
2 cups or 480 g tofu
1/3 cup or 85 ml sunflower oil
1/2 cup or 125 ml maple syrup or honey
1 1/2 tsp. or 5 ml corn starch
1 1/2 tsp. or 5 ml vanilla
3 tbsp. or 30 ml cocoa powder
A pinch of salt

Preheat the oven to 350 degrees F (175 degrees C).

Mix all the ingredients in a mixer at medium setting until a creamy consistency is obtained.

Pour the mixture into the pie shell and bake in the oven for 30 minutes, or just until your finger does not stick to the filling.

Cool down for 20 minutes before placing in the refrigerator.

VARIATION:
Carob may be used instead of cocoa.

Tofu cheese pie (North America)

By SÉBASTIEN LEBLOND

Degree of difficulty*
Cost $
For 4 people

PIE CRUST:
1 1/2 slices soft part of whole wheat bread
1/4 cup or 65 ml powdered milk, not instant
1 tbsp. or 15 ml baking powder
1 tbsp. or 15 ml rolled oats
1 tbsp. or 15 ml ground unshelled sesame seeds
1/4 cup or 65 ml safflower oil
1 tbsp. or 15 ml honey

Break up the bread and add the powdered milk, unshelled ground sesame seeds and the rolled oats. Mix.

Add, little by little, the oil and honey. Set aside.

FILLING:
3/4 cup or 200 ml extra firm silken tofu
1/4 cup or 65 ml sour cream
1 cup or 250 ml cottage cheese
2 eggs
1/4 cup or 65 ml honey
1/4 cup or 65 ml light wheat flour
1 tsp. vanilla
Peel of 1/2 lemon

Preheat the oven to 350 degrees F (175 degrees C).
Mix the tofu, cheese and sour cream in a blender.
Add the eggs, honey, flour and vanilla. Remove from the blender.

Add the lemon peels and mix. Set aside.
Grease a 9 inch or 23 cm pie plate and spread the crust mixture on the bottom of the plate.
Pour the mixture onto the pie crust and bake for 30 minutes.
Cool. Serve with cherry jam.

Divine!

A fresh breeze of cantaloupe (Quebec)

By SYLVIE TROTTIER

"An amazing recipe, one of the treasures of "La Magie du tofu!"

Degree of difficulty*
Cost $
For 2 people

2 cups or 500 ml cantaloupe*
1/2 cup or 125 ml cold pressed apple juice
100 ml silken tofu

Place all the ingredients in a mixer.

Serve immediately.

*Cantaloupe is the name given in North America for melon brodé.

Summer smoothie (United States)

By JEAN GRENIER

"Refreshing, dynamic, to have at the waterside!"

- Frances Boyte

Degree of difficulty*
Cost $
For 4 people

1/2 cup or 125 ml fresh strawberries
1/2 cup or 125 ml fresh raspberries
1/2 cup or 125 ml fresh blueberries
1 apple cut into quarters
1 Asian pear
4 ounces or 125 ml fresh orange juice
2 ice cubes
1/2 cup or 125 ml silken tofu

Place all ingredients in a blender and mix well.

Jean Grenier, a fashion designer for 26 years and a clothing sculptor, has a new passion for tofu. Jean Grenier's philosophy: it is not worth running to fashion, you simply have to walk to a style: your own

Stilton fruit and cheese

By JOSÉ TROTTIER

"Be sure to make a large quantity as you will be asked for more! Marvelous! It brings back London."
- Frances Boyte

Degree of difficulty*

Cost $$

For 4 people

1/2 cup or 125 ml dry white wine or white port
1/4 cup or 65 ml crumbled Stilton cheese
1/2 cup or 125 ml silken soft tofu
1 tbsp. honey
4 bowls small mixed fruit
       (blueberries, bilberries, raspberries)

Preheat the oven to grill.

Place the wine and the cheese in a pan and melt the cheese.

Add the tofu and honey. Mix well.

If necessary, keep cooking the sauce to reduce it to a thick consistency.

Cover the fruit with this mixture.

Place under the grill until the sauce has a light colour.

Serve as soon as possible.

Fresh fruit kabobs with chocolate (Quebec)

By DIDIER GIROL

Degree of difficulty*
Cost $
For 6 to 8 people

TOFU SAUCE:
1/2 cup or 100 g silken tofu
1/4 cup or 50 g fresh well-ripened strawberry purée
1/4 cup or 50 g fructose

Mix all these ingredients. Set aside.

CHOCOLATE SAUCE:
3/4 cup or 100 g black chocolate 72% cocoa
3 tbsp. or 45 ml hot water
3 drops orange essential oil

*Keep the orange peel and squeeze it over the chocolate sauce. This is the orange essential oil. Even not distilled, it gives all the flavour! It is the same thing with a lemon. Try this practice and delight.

AT TIME OF SERVING:
In a small bowl, melt the chocolate over hot water.
Add the water and orange essential oil.

KEBOBS:
1 banana
6 strawberries
1 kiwi
6 large grapes
1 apple
1 orange
6 cubes firm tofu

Peel and slice the banana into 6 portions.

Wash, hull and cut the strawberries in half.

Peel the kiwi and cut in half lengthwise and then each half into 3 portions.

Wash the grapes.

Peel and cut the apple into 6 large pieces.

Peel the orange and keep the skin. Cut out the white part of the skin all around the orange with a very sharp, small knife, then remove the sections (the pieces of orange without skin). Keep the best 6 sections.

Place the fruit on 6 skewers, alternating the fruit with the cubes of tofu.

Set aside the fresh kebobs.

When ready to serve, prepare the chocolate sauce.

Cover the bottom of each plate with the tofu sauce, place the kebob and drizzle with the chocolate sauce while it is still warm.

Decorate with a leaf of fresh mint.

This recipe is adapted from the book, "La santé au dessert", published by Éditions Multimondes by the master pastry chef and teacher at the health and tourism Center in Quebec, Didier Girol.

"After 32 years as a pastry chef (talk about a career that is dangerous for the waistline), I have finally managed to return all the pleasure and the taste in my collection of recipes. But how, you might ask? I took it upon myself to talk to a dietician. Suzanne Beaulieu has pulled off miracles. She is no friend of the hard core fans of sugar. All the same, we can open the door to future generations of pastry chefs for them to understand that it is possible for the words dessert and health to co-exist. How does tofu fit into all this? There is no better place to find it than in a healthful recipe."

-Didier Girol

Index